THE LAST OF THE GOOD GIRLS

BELLEVUE, WASHINGTON

the last
of the
good girls

**Shedding Convention,
Coming Out Whole**

By

MARY ANN WOODRUFF

Foreword by Rev. Chris Glaser

Text Copyright © 2013 by Mary Ann Woodruff
Poetry Copyright © 2013 Mary Ann Woodruff
Cover Art Copyright © 2013 by Mary Ann Woodruff

All rights reserved.
No part of this book may be reproduced in any form by any means
without the express permission of the author.

Cover and Interior Design: Kathryn Campbell
Cover Photo: Sycamores, Mount Holyoke College, 1957/Mary Ann Woodruff
Author Photo: Studio Vogue

The Last of the Good Girls: Shedding Convention, Coming Out Whole
ISBN-10: 1490552960
ISBN-13: 978-1490552965

LCCN 2013912298

Printed in the United States of America by CreateSpace
Published in the United States of America by
Moon Day Press, Bellevue, Washington

For

*my daughter Katie,
whose 101 questions got me started;*

my son Jim, whose comments made the writing better;

*my grandchildren Rita, Kurt, Jamie, and Tess,
who deserve the story;*

my sister Jean, for a lifetime of support; and

*Bob and Mary,
from whom I have learned so much about love
and myself.*

Contents

Foreword ix

Prologue 1

The Big Question 5

East Coast 9

Midwest 43

Pacific Northwest 59

Breaking Out 73

Pulling Apart 97

Going In 133

Coming Out 161

Epilogue 187

Acknowledgments 191

Foreword

THIS ENGAGING, heartfelt memoir quotes Judith Barrington from a 1993 poetry workshop: "The poet's job is to write the truth. And then write the truth below the truth." That is precisely what Mary Ann Woodruff has done in often lyrical prose and occasional poetry. She did it first with her life, discovering truth under truth, and now with this remarkable book. A life well-lived deserves a story well-told such as this.

Set against carefully detailed American horizons of the Northeast, the Midwest, and ultimately the Northwest, Woodruff traces her interior horizons from model homemaker, mother, and wife to successful consultant, deeper realized self, and a new experience of home—with herself, with supportive women, and finally with another woman.

Like Jacob, the subject of one of her poems, she struggles with a God who might judge her as she has judged herself, and wrestles with both a church and a culture in which she nonetheless gladly played her assigned and chosen roles. She contends with her identity and calling without abandoning those she loves, including her husband and children and even the Presbyterian Church. Instead she brings them along, just as they, by their own love, bring her along, though the church fumbles and stumbles. The reader is drawn into this circle of intimacy and love, cheering her on even as she welcomes the reader along. My heart was opened, and I was left with happy tears.

This is the way our stories should be told, not with a demand to agree, but with an invitation to understanding. Mary Ann's lifelong process encourages us to gently contemplate our own lives, what hidden truths underlie the truths we live for others, what we need to claim personally and proclaim publicly, how we have, in the words of her favored Psalm 139, been "awesomely and wonderfully" but also *uniquely* made by a God who loves us unconditionally.

One of Mary Ann's most moving poems is entitled "Gratitude," a wondering litany of creative images that begins:

I wonder.
Does a tree trunk thank the leaves
for shading her roots, for the miracle
of photosynthesis that gives her life?

In gratitude for Mary Ann Woodruff's *The Last of the Good Girls: Shedding Convention, Coming Out Whole,* I too wonder:

Do her words thank the author
for stringing them like Christmas bulbs
to light the reader's way to a new Advent?

Chris Glaser

Atlanta

Rev. Chris Glaser is the author of a dozen books, the first being *Uncommon Calling: A Gay Christian's Struggle to Serve the Church.* He blogs weekly reflections for progressive Christians at http://chrisglaser.blogspot.com.

Prologue

IT IS MORNING IN SEATTLE, Thursday, June 10, 2010. Nine fifteen, to be exact. I'm on time, in the Starbucks on the corner of Sixth and Union: smooth jazz, whoosh of espresso machine, metallic rattle of bean grinders, click-click of a coffee basket being filled, dark-roasted hints of Brazil and Kenya into the air. Commuters dash in bearing briefcases and furrowed brows, walk out with fingers wrapped around hot paper cups of relief. At a table by the window, a man in a gray sports shirt frowns at the *Seattle Times*—how far has the Gulf oil spill spread today?

I walk to the table where Bob Woodruff sits. He looks up: big smile, crinkly hazel eyes, white hair, open face. "I got here early." His voice rises above the cacophony. "I've got a new Orca pass and took the bus." That's Bob, ready for anything.

I drop my coat and go for my own drink. "Double-tall non-fat wet cappuccino in a for-here cup," the cashier calls to the barista. I collect my change and go to the end of the counter, where it is ready–shiny foam, with a coffee-colored heart sculpted on top. Mmm. I inhale the fragrance.

I return to the table where Bob sits and settle into my chair. His new green sweater nearly bounces with energy. What does he see, looking at me? Graying hair past due for the 10:30 cut that follows this get-together? New red raincoat, familiar smile, blue eyes, peaceful spirit?

We have met, as we do frequently, to check in about our grandchildren. We've both visited the two in Portland recently, and that is always worth a conversation.

"Do you know where we were thirty-five years ago today?" Bob begins.

"No," I say. "Where?"

"We were in Amsterdam finding out that Dad had just died. We were figuring out how to interrupt our trip to fly to Florida. We landed in that terrible thunderstorm, remember? We never got to the Danish coast."

Of course I remember now. The Pulitzer Hotel, the place where the ruddy-faced American man in the camel-hair jacket stood in the lobby, bellowing, "Jeez, we gave these people the Marshall Plan. For all we've done, you'd think that at least when we come over here there would be better…" We never could remember what it was he'd wanted to be better, because we just tried to get out of there, fast. Then in our room, hearing Bob's end of the phone call from his secretary, crushing into a towel the slacks I had just washed, bouncing up and down on the bundle to get it dried in a hurry, packing, leaving, flying the long, long journey to Fort Myers. Yes, I remember. The shock of the unexpected, the aftershock of the way his mother dealt with it. We breathe. Hoke Smith Woodruff was a good man.

"By the way"—Bob moves on, cheerfully—"Happy nearly fiftieth anniversary!"

Ah. I remembered that before I got here. June 25, 1960, a hot day in Rochester, New York. The all-American girl and the boy next door, joining hands and promising, "till death do us part." Bob and I are silent. The mystery of it all, I think.

"You know," he says, "it's really OK. But sometimes—I miss you." His hazel eyes are moist on mine.

I nod. "It *is* OK." I nod again. "And sometimes—I miss you, too."

We sit, in the middle of Starbucks on the corner of Sixth and Union in downtown Seattle, sudden tears filling both our eyes.

The Big Question

Chapter 1

How does one compose a life? Some would say it is a matter of intention, of self-determination. I have met people who say they always wanted to be a doctor or always knew they were gay. I have met people who say they've just muddled along, putting one foot in front of the other, doing the next thing. Some are propelled by a vision, some strive to escape pain. Others might say life is simply a glorious experiment.

I've given this a great deal of thought as I've put together what I call this necklace of narrative strung with beads of poetry. I want to draw a map for you of my own life's twists and turns and tell you, at times, what I've made of it. I've tried to answer my own question: How did I get here? How did a nice, conventional good girl like me grow up… and up… and up… to be… queer?

How I Got Here

>If you ask me how I got here
>I might shrug and say, search me;
>I might say
>life's a mystery;
>I might say

I walked through some open doors
and not others;
I might say
now and then I get a glimpse
of the other side of my life's tapestry,
the side away from the slubs,
knots, and loose threads I see most of the time,
and that when I do,
I sometimes think I see a pattern.

But all of these would be half-truths.

The truth—I know this now—
is that I was drawn,
as surely as the full moon pulls the tides,
to the shores of some vast ocean
and that her depths, swells,
rages, and exquisite calms
are home to me.

If you ask me how I got here
I'd say I turned one day
and headed home.

East Coast

Chapter 2

IT IS A MUGGY MORNING *in June, 1935. Ruth Sparklin has bid her husband, Jimmy, good-bye as he leaves for work. They have recently moved to Rochester, New York, from Delaware, leaving all their close family and friends behind, for this job of my father's at a machine tool company owned by the husband of Ruth's mother's cousin. They are living in a small apartment on East Avenue, the elm-lined street that goes downtown to the center of Rochester in one direction and out through the suburbs of Brighton and Pittsford to the Erie Canal in the other.*

Ruth dresses her two-year-old daughter, Jean, in a sunsuit and takes her behind the apartment building to the playground, where a swing and sandbox are ready for children. Sitting Jean on the swing, she provides a few desultory shoves to set her in motion. Jean dangles her feet and chirps with pleasure as she watches her toes wriggling below her. Ruth's mind wanders as she gazes around her.

The large brick building and evergreen trees make for a cool playground, but dark. Accustomed to the bright flatlands of southern Delaware, the ubiquitous aroma of chicken farm and salt air, she wrinkles her nose at the scent of evergreen. Where has she landed? Who is this man, her husband, so driven—by fear?

she wonders—that he jumps up, dresses in silence, eats breakfast without noticing what she's prepared, and dashes off to his new job with a quick peck at the side of her cheek? No lingering in the sleepy warmth of bed, snuggling their daughter between them, not this morning nor, she realizes in her stomach, since they arrived that night two months ago, worn from the rough road and their own anxiety to settle into the apartment prepared by Cousin Elizabeth.

All of the above is invented. My sister and I have spent years trying to understand our mother. What I know is this: it is time to move past being afraid of her. The fact that I didn't get to this until the threshold of my sixtieth year is not all my fault.

When I was a kid, I loved the candy called Good and Plenty. A pack of Good and Plenty, pink and white bullets wrapped around licorice centers, could keep you going through a double feature at Lowe's Theater. It strikes me now that Good and Plenty is a perfect metaphor for the rules that governed my growing up, indeed framed nearly the first fifty years of my life. If you were Good, there would be Plenty. It was as simple and as complicated as that.

I grew up in Plenty. My parents did not. My father, James Sparklin, was the only son of a Methodist parson and a dynamo of a missionary woman whose vocation had taken her to the far reaches of America's Southwest before she met my grandfather and gave up her calling to join his. Grandpa Sparklin ministered to one small town after another in Delaware; my father and his sisters changed schools nearly every year, because they moved that often. That was the Methodist way. Grandpa's pay was more often a chicken for the family of six to share of a Sunday than money. My father and his sisters were raised as proper preacher's kids: no movies, no dancing. That, too, was the Methodist way.

My mother, Ruth Melson, grew up on a farm in lower Delaware, outside the small town of Bridgeville. She was the elder daughter of a father who had dropped out of school in sixth grade and a sweet mother, who pretty much disappeared into the kitchen of her in-laws who owned the farm. They, too, were Methodists.

My parents met at the University of Delaware, from which they graduated in the late twenties. Jimmy, as he was called by his friends, was a handsome fraternity man with the cachet of having spent a year at the US Naval Academy, including a midshipmen's cruise to Europe. Ruth was a bob-haired flapper and home economics major.

They married in 1931, in the lean time of the Great Depression. At first they lived near Wilmington, Delaware, in a bungalow across the lane from Edge Moor Iron Works, where my father worked. My mother taught high-school home economics until my sister was due.

My sister, Jean, was born in 1933. Soon after that, rumors started that my father's company was about to be liquidated, and the family went to work to "save Jimmy." Mother's mother's Cousin Elizabeth had married a man who had a machine tool company in Rochester, New York, and Cousin Alfred offered my father a job as a sales engineer. My father grabbed the opportunity, trading ties of family and friends for a lifeline of financial security. After he moved his family to Rochester, my father stayed with Consolidated Machine Tool until he retired and prided himself that he had never had a day without work.

My mother's cousins, Elizabeth and Alfred Trosch, took my parents under their wings, advised them on where they should live, and held the mortgage for the house in the suburb of Brighton they bought in 1941 and lived in for fifty years. It was a good investment;

I'm sure my parents never missed a payment, and our part of Brighton, with its excellent schools and affordable houses, would always be a popular place for first-home buyers.

More than bankers, the Trosches were our family—the only family we had outside of Delaware. If my parents chafed under the burden of owing so much to Cousin Elizabeth and Cousin Alfred, I never felt it. It seemed to me that we were lucky to have family near, and Cousin Elizabeth and Cousin Alfred were like grandparents to Jean and me. Both of my parents' mothers died the year I was born; Cousin Elizabeth was like a second mother to mine, a daily phone connection to what she knew best and cared about most deeply. Every summer, we drove to Delaware to visit our relatives, traveling from grandfather to grandfather, aunt to aunt, cousins to cousins. Though we lived in Rochester, I think that for my parents, Delaware was always home.

We celebrated all holidays with the Trosches and saw a lot of them in between. Cousin Elizabeth and Cousin Alfred lived in one of the more well-to-do sections of Brighton, fitting for the family of a man who owned a successful company. I know we learned a lot about what well-to-do meant through them, what Good people did, had, and thought. But as a child I mostly just saw magic. They had a back stairway from their kitchen that joined the main one on a landing halfway up the stairs. They had a glider swing on their screened-in porch. There were tiny salt dishes next to each person's place setting at their table for dinner. They set up a miniature Swiss village under their Christmas tree, and I spent part of every Christmas Day on my stomach surveying all the treasures in that village. I sat next to Cousin Elizabeth at church in the winter and stroked the fox pelts that chased each others' tails around the shoulders of her coat.

Cousin Elizabeth and Cousin Alfred had two daughters, some fifteen years older than my sister and me, who were role models for us. Janet and Margie were a lot of fun, always full of stories and adventures. After college, they each went on to amazing careers—Janet worked in New York for *LIFE* magazine, Margie sang in the Metropolitan Opera Company. They lived in the Barbizon Hotel for Women, the only appropriate place in Cousin Elizabeth's eyes, where no men were allowed above the first floor, and strict dress and conduct codes prevailed. The Trosch girls played a lot of bridge with our parents, games lubricated with Cokes, laughter, and conversation; I hung around as much as I could so I could visit with whoever was the dummy during their games. I saw my first opera, *La Boheme*, with Margie, in Rochester's Highland Park Bowl, when I was in college.

* * *

My parents waited until they felt solid about their economic future before having a second child, and they were sure that child would be a boy. A curly-haired athletic tyke with a red baseball cap, "John Walter" lived in their imagination for months. Surprise! I was born in June, 1938. Mother feared my father would be disappointed at having another girl. When she awakened in the hospital, she often told me with great pride, there was a big bouquet of flowers by her bed and this note: "She's beautiful and I love you. Jimmy." Still, I was a week old before they recovered from their shock and named me: Mary for my mother's mother, Mary Simpson Melson; Ann for my father's mother, Anna Rodrigues Sparklin.

Regardless of name or gender, I toddled after my father from early on and in many ways became the son he longed for. I learned baseball from my father—how to throw like a boy, how to score games at Silver Stadium where the AAA Red Wings played. I picked up grass on Saturdays when he cut it and, when we were done, had my own four-ounce cheese glass full of beer with him. While my sister learned sewing and tailoring from Mother, I learned woodworking and barbershop harmony from Daddy.

I was three and my sister Jean was eight that first December weekend of 1941 when we moved to our new house on the corner of Landing and Kimbark Roads in Brighton. Pictures of that period show the house barely finished, surrounded by snow and mud, Jean and me in snowsuits, Mother and Daddy in coats and hats (no decent woman went anywhere without a hat). Our house was the first or second built in a new development on Kimbark Road, and the other homes were like ours: wood with some stone trim, two stories, three bedrooms, one bath. If you were really lucky, as we were, you had a bath and a half, which meant you had a teeny powder room on the first floor. Those homes filled as quickly as they were built. The postwar white rush to the suburbs had not started yet, but these were good houses in what we would call now an upwardly mobile part of Brighton, and they attracted a rush of their own.

Each of the houses had a new tree in the front yard. Our house had a large blue spruce in the front yard and a linden tree on the side facing Kimbark, where our driveway was. That linden tree came to be my hideout as I grew big enough to climb. My best friend Terry—she moved into the neighborhood in sixth grade—and I used to climb that tree. We would carry a peck basket up behind us, in which we had stashed peanut-butter sandwiches and Nancy Drew mysteries. We would each find a comfortable crotch in the tree and read the languid summer afternoons away.

Life was simple in the neighborhood of my childhood. The mothers were at home all day; the fathers drove shiny black Fords or Chevrolets into their driveways around 5:30 each evening, where the wives would have dinner, or at least the newspaper, ready. As I grew up, there was always a pack of kids to play with when school was out. We were roustabouts, free to run loose outside, free to be children. Any parent on the block could discipline any child; we all knew everyone. I was a tomboy, as were most of my girlfriends. One of our family stories centers around a pink coat and bonnet Mother made me one year for Easter. My father took my picture in it just as I announced, "I can beat up everyone in my class except for Hermie Judd."

Whatever sensuality I experienced when I was a kid came from being outdoors. The smells of outdoors even now take me back to childhood... freshly mown grass under our our backs as we imagined pictures in the clouds, the crisp metallic scent of winter air laden with unborn snow, the dusky aroma of burning leaves in fall. The feel of outdoors, too—warm sun on my hair while riding my bike, summer rains pelting our shoulders as we ran about jumping in puddles, the scritch of asphalt streets on bare feet, the sweaty wrestling we were prone to, tumbling over and over with a joyous, competitive physicality. The sounds of outdoors ring in my dreams—rhythmic music of chains on passing cars breaking the quiet after snowfall, the click-clack of marbles shooting across circles drawn in the dirt, the slap of jump ropes on the pavement in spring, the incessant buzz of locusts on summer afternoons, the cheers of our gang at One-A-Cat or Red Rover on Kimbark Road, the echo of our mothers calling us inside at dark. My mouth still carries the tastes of outdoors—nectar sucked from honeysuckle blossoms, potato chips we fried on tin-can stoves in Sue Spiehler's backyard, homemade ice cream licked off the batters of the churn on Memorial Day. Remembered sights of childhood outdoors get me through dental appointments now—fresh snow dazzling in the sun just before a game of Fox and Geese, water, diverted by our snow dams, rushing this way and that down the edges of the street, brilliant yellow skunk cabbage announcing spring in the ravine, fireflies we caught in canning jars at dusk. The outdoor world was safe, with just an edge of adventure, a banquet of abundance, and we partook fully of it.

Indoors was different. Indoors was my mother. She could go from quiet, even shy, to furious and violent in an instant. Jean and I never figured out what caused her tempers. Many a Monday washday she would stomp up the basement steps, toting the clothes basket to the backyard, where she stabbed clothespins into place and huffed indignation into the air. She carried on furious conversations with invisible adversaries, sotto voce soliloquies that left my sister and me staring wide-eyed at each other. Inside, she hissed dissatisfaction into the houseplants, spitting barely contained rage, rehearsing arguments with people who needed to be straightened out.

It was only after Mother's death, in her eighties, that I heard the story of the beatings she gave my sister when she was little. Jean said once Mother beat her so hard that Daddy cried.

"How old were you?" I stammered.

"Oh, probably about seven," Jean said.

I'm sure I witnessed some of this, though I have no conscious recall. But I became a little charmer, attentive to my mother's emotional swings, anticipating, working to be whatever I thought she wanted or needed me to be. Indoors, I knew that my safety, my very life, depended on staying on her good side. I was so attuned to my mother's feelings that I wasn't aware I had any. I learned early that the best way to get along in life was to be good, very good. If I was Good, I got Plenty—of affection, and peace. If I was bad, she could stalk to the poplar tree at the edge of our property, strip the leaves from a sucker, and start switching my legs quicker than I could get out of the way.

Indoors, I was wary, my eyes constantly on the barometer that was my mother's moods. Outdoors, I was free, and I chose outdoors whenever I could. All of this was utterly unconscious at the time. I only became aware of this through years of therapy, beginning in my fifties.

* * *

World War II was a backdrop to my early childhood. The attack on Pearl Harbor occurred the weekend we moved into our house in Brighton. Because I was young, I remember only sparse details: singing with Cousin Alfred, "Don't Sit Under the Apple Tree with Anyone Else but Me;" my father, too old to go to war, taking his air raid warden helmet from the top shelf of the hall closet when sirens sounded; going out in the victory garden off Atlantic Boulevard, where we went most evenings after dinner; playing at the edges of the garden with Jean while Mother and Daddy worked the soil and weeded. What crops we had! In August, Mother put up fresh vegetables and fruits that lasted us all through the winters, filling the kitchen with aromas of fresh tomatoes, chili sauce, peaches, beans, blackberry currant jelly, and strawberry jam, sweat pouring off her face in the humid heat of Rochester summers. Jean and I got into terrible trouble the day we loaded up our little red wagon with extra zucchini and went door-to-door trying to sell them to neighbors, who had their own overloads of zucchini.

When I got whooping cough the whole family was quarantined,

and gas rationing meant we couldn't even go for a ride in the '37 Pontiac, the black one with the running boards, to break the monotony. I remember going with Mother to our local grocery store and watching her count out coupons for sugar; mixing the red capsule into the white oleo to make it yellow; stomping tin cans to flatten them. Everything was for the "war effort," even my parents rolling their own cigarettes on a little contraption my father brought home. Mother taught Jean and her classmates how to knit, then sewed all their raggedy eight-inch squares into blankets to send to the front. The war came to our home in *LIFE* magazine, which we would all pore over, studying photos and reading the stories. It came close as well on D-Day, June 6, 1944, not only because it was my sixth birthday, but also because my twenty-something cousin Janet Trosch sent a cryptic telegram to let the family know that she had sailed that day on the Queen Mary to join the Red Cross Clubmobile in Europe. She would pass out coffee and donuts behind the lines as the Allies made their way into France.

* * *

Our parents said they'd had enough religion as children to last a lifetime. All that country Methodism had worn them down—vespers on Wednesday nights, Sunday school and church on Sunday, plus, for my father, riding the buckboard with his father to a different rural church each Sunday night for an extra service. Still, they considered it important that we were exposed to religion, and they moved from denomination to denomination, never satisfied with any minister for long. Jean settled at Asbury First Methodist when she joined their youth group; I got attached to Brighton Presbyterian, which our parents joined when I was a teen. Church mattered to the two of us. It was a mystery to my father, he said years later, that Jean and I got to be so "churchy."

Regardless of how our parents felt about church, we said grace at every meal in our home, Grandpa Sparklin's preacher cadence echoing in my father's voice:

Accept our thanks, our Heavenly Father, for these and all Thy mercies. Use them for the good of our bodies and our lives in Thy service. In His name we ask it, Amen.

My grandfather's grace ended with "For Christ's sake, Amen." But early on, my sister Jean picked up the phrase "for Christ's sake!" as a handy exclamation to use around the house. By the time I came along, our table grace had been modified.

* * *

Sexual awareness was not part of my childhood. In the buttoned-up world that was marriage as I observed it in my parents, there was affection—I never saw my father leave for work or return home without a kiss with my mother, and we'd be spellbound when, on occasion, they would dance around the living room—but nothing in their behavior so much as hinted at passion. My father was a modest man. I never saw him naked or downstairs in a bathrobe. He preferred twin beds, so they had twin beds. Mother's irritation lay just below the surface and could explode at me or my sister without warning, but I never saw it directed at my father. They never fought, ever, although sometimes a silence could last for days.

My mother seemed naïve or mortified about things related to the body. Once I was grounded for days when I yelled "Shit!" as we drove through a big puddle. I was imitating what I heard when the water splashed on the windshield and was shocked when Mother got furious and made me stay in my own yard for days as punishment. Even when the punishment was over, I was still asking her what I had done wrong. "That was a very bad word," she said. When I pressed her, she told me that shit meant urination.

When I was in sixth grade, she asked, blushing, if I had hair "down there." She was pleased when our Girl Scout troop saw *Very Personally Yours*, the movie explaining menstruation, and I remember her and Jean waiting for me when I got home that day and asking me what I thought about it. While she was ready with sanitary pads and a belt when I needed them, we never had "the talk." What I learned about sex I learned from the slightly older girls in the neighborhood one day standing under the linden tree in our yard. My reaction was disbelief: "They do what?!"

I don't remember hearing anything about homosexuality as a child. For years when I was young, a professor from McGill University in Montreal joined our family for Christmas. He was a friend of Janet and Margie Trosch, a man they had met in Mexico while they were all studying Spanish. Leonard was a great conversationalist, debonair, witty—and gay as they come. No one remarked on this, at least not in my hearing.

* * *

In so many ways, my childhood was idyllic. The freedom of outdoors was enchanting. The stability of life in our neighborhood and our school was reassuring. Americans were the good guys who had saved the world in the war, and pride in our country and respect for its leaders made a deep impression. Yet my mother's tempers cast a longer shadow. Once someone asked if I had a vivid image of childhood. "Yes," I answered without missing a beat, "I'm a little kid cringing in a corner." Being Good exacted a price I would pay for years.

Chapter 3

ROCHESTER, NEW YORK, is an upstate city bounded by Lake Ontario to the north, the former Erie Canal to the south, Irondequoit Bay to the east, and a highway to Niagara Falls to the west. And bounded as well, in the forties and fifties of my coming of age, by tight convention.

Rochester was not unique in this conventionality; the postwar period was defined by conformity across the country. We children attended public schools that looked the same all across the country. A, a, B, b, C, c, etc., marched across the border of every classroom wall in the nation, George Washington's level gaze observed the same rows of wooden/iron desks bolted in parallel rows to the floor, children pledged allegiance to the same American flag at the start of each and every school day. Our mothers kept house with an eye to *Good Housekeeping* or *The Ladies Home Journal* for instructions in how to do it properly, while work was the sole purview of fathers. This last may speak of classism; our families were lucky in that none of the mothers had to work outside the home.

Rochester was a white-collar city of clean industry. Eastman Kodak, Xerox (known until 1958 as the Haloid Photography Company), Bausch & Lomb, Gleason Works, Taylor Instrument, Stromberg Carlson, these companies required educated leaders, whose lives were meant to be orderly—at least in the upper-middle-class neighborhoods like Brighton where the men who ran those companies dwelled with their families.

Social mores that maintained order were quietly understood and as quietly enforced. Each golf or social club, for example, had its own clearly defined constituency. Old money belonged to and played golf at the Country Club of Rochester, Jews belonged to Irondequoit Country Club, newer money to Oak Hill, while Monroe was a "middle ground" golf club where couples like Cousin Elizabeth and Cousin Alfred, who didn't play golf, could have a social membership and be proud to take guests for dinner. The Century Club was where upper-crust matrons, whose families had been Rochesterians for generations, went for lunch; the Chatterbox Club hosted parties and dances for the smart set, including an annual holiday SnowBall, to which my friends and I were invited throughout college. While there was plenty of money in Rochester, it was considered gauche to show it. Anything nouveau riche was frowned upon—or more likely, met with a slightly raised eyebrow that said it all. *Smugtown, USA*, written by one of my friends' fathers and published in 1957, was a scathing critique of Rochester society that appalled everyone, probably because it was so on the mark.

My parents made it possible, through frugality and our cousins' help in buying a home in Brighton, for Jean and me to grow up in this upper-middle-class Plenty. They also did us the great favor of leveling with us about our family's economic reality. "You'll always find people around you who have more money than you do, so you'd best get comfortable with it," they advised. "And"—they were quick to add—"if you look around, you will always find people who have a whole lot less." Mother sewed nearly all of our clothes. Impulse purchases were out of the question. We came to understand that a comment by either parent, "Oh, I don't think we need that," might mean we didn't need it, but more often was code for "we can't afford it."

Our family went to the library once a week; we all came home with armloads of books. I dropped off to sleep most nights to the voices of my parents in the living room downstairs, where they read and talked until the 11:00 news came on the big floor model Philco. The one luxury we had was an upright piano. My father taught himself to play, all on the black keys. Mother would occasionally thump out one of the old Methodist hymns. When we showed interest, Jean and I both had piano lessons.

I would never have been invited to "come out" as a debutante, but I had friends who did. I still remember the night I left for a debutante party at which one of my friends was being presented to society. "Just remember," my father said with a twinkle in his eye as I paused by the door, "when you get there, *you're* out." We both laughed.

The public schools in Brighton were excellent. Thirty-six of us started kindergarten at Indian Landing School and went through eighth grade together. Rochester was famous for the Eastman School of Music, and Indian Landing was fortunate to have an excellent music program. We all started playing violins in second grade—even if someone wanted to play trumpet, he started on violin—all of us sawing away on half- or three-quarter-size instruments rented from school. We had a school orchestra that was the envy of the county; often we'd play for other schools interested in starting their own orchestra.

In ninth grade, we were bused to Brighton High School, joining a much larger cohort of classmates who had been on the high-school campus since seventh grade. We were ready for high-school academics, thanks to excellent grade-school teachers. Socially, however we were blissfully unprepared.

Having a boyfriend at Indian Landing meant having someone special to play and talk with. Kent Mook, the love of my seventh- and eighth-grade life, came to dinner at my house, invited me to movies with his mother and father. Our parents dutifully enrolled us in dancing class in eighth grade, so we'd be ready for the sock hops and dances that were a big part of high-school life. Imagine our shock, then, at the first back-to-school dance in high school. Kent and I, Indian Landing newbies, danced our perfect fox-trot squares—and at arm's length—only to observe our classmates, who'd been watching upperclassmen for two years. They were pressed together in tight embraces, swaying slowly to the music. This was a crash course in teen sophistication, and one we were determined to pass.

Picking up the cues for what kept one safe as a teenager was easy after a childhood of watching for my mother's moods. At Brighton High School, the rules for Good girls were clear: be smart—but not too smart—and be popular. That wasn't too hard for me, though I remember dizzily morphing from one persona to the next. I was a serious student tapped for the National Honor Society as a junior; part of the fun clique who never missed a slumber party; a thespian who ran with the theater crowd; a member of a trio who sang at dances. And on occasion, I joined the girls who hung out behind the school smoking at the end of lunch hour. I went steady with a classmate who was New York State amateur golf champion; I was elected secretary of student government in my sophomore year, then refused to run for president when nominated in my junior year, because no girl had ever been president, and I couldn't upstage the golf champion. Being Good led to Plenty; being too Good would be risky business.

I had little idea of how I felt or what I really thought about anything. Fitting in was much more important than finding out. I could keep cadence with any group that mattered; it didn't occur to me I had a self with whom to be in step.

I did know one thing: there was Something bigger than I, and that Something was important to me, called to me. As high-school juniors, several friends and I spent a summer week at Westminster Park, a Presbyterian camp in the Thousand Islands. Perched on a rock high above the Saint Lawrence River at sunset one night, I listened to quiet singing nearby while taking in the beauty all around me. This is perfect, I thought. This spot, these people, this music, this peace. This is God—here, all around me. I want this with me, always.

The rules around sex were also embodied in Good and Plenty: nice girls didn't. Going too far was not Good, and would get you in Plenty of trouble. Oh, there was a lot of fumbling around in the back seats of cars, to be sure, necking at the drive-in, petting at favorite sites in Ellison Park or along the Erie Canal. But none of us could bear the thought of standing pregnant before our parents. Birth-control pills would be introduced in 1960, the year I graduated from college. Before then, in the precarious balance between exploration and inhibition there was no protection available to passionate good girls that could be counted on to prevent pregnancy. It made sense, then, for girls to hold the line.

As I was finishing high school, I had my first date with Bob Woodruff. He had graduated from Brighton High two years ahead of me, though I first met him when he came to my house to paint posters for the student council campaign when I ran for secretary ("No Malarky, Vote for Sparky!"). Now he had just completed his sophomore year in college. What struck me immediately was that when I couldn't go out with him the first time he called, he stayed on the phone, talking easily. When we finally connected for our first date, I came home and told my mother I would probably marry him. He was fun to be with, interested in everything, comfortable in his own skin, and a good conversationalist. He was the kind of person who never met a stranger. He had hazel eyes and wore glasses. He had been a lifeguard and taught swimming to half the younger kids in Brighton. When he trained his easy confidence on me, I was smitten. In September I went off to Mount Holyoke College in South Hadley, Massachusetts, and he returned to Colgate in Hamilton, New York. We burned up the miles between us with letters, phone calls, and visits.

Mount Holyoke was a seminal experience for me. A women's college, it offered me four years (1956–1960) of freedom to explore my strengths that I hadn't felt before, when it seemed so important not to outshine boys. I had watched my brilliant mother working her southern wiles to make sure that every smart idea came out of my father's mouth; I had a lifetime of acquired assumptions to be challenged. At Mount Holyoke, classes were fascinating. Ideas flew fast and furiously, my college friends were as bright or brighter than I, and women professors and administrators provided life-changing role models. They were wise, witty, realized women, uninhibited by the role expectations I brought to campus with me. I was encouraged to be and do all that I could, to try things without fear of failure, to delight in triumphs—my own and those of other women. I delved into intellectual disciplines that still fascinate me: the great questions and ideas found in English literature, religion, history, music—appreciation, performance, and composition. I reveled in the sheer beauty of the New England campus, two lakes reflecting brilliant foliage every fall, acres of peace in which to walk and reflect. Friendships made at

Mount Holyoke were deep and lasting. We played bridge endlessly, dissected films like *Wild Strawberries* deep into the night, discussed everything. For me, attending Mount Holyoke for college was like being outdoors as a kid—freeing, joyous, expansive.

Bob and I discussed our intentions about sexual intercourse. We were committed to waiting for marriage, Bob as much as I, and we knew that in my parents' eyes that meant waiting until I graduated. Bob was a charter member of Twelve Corners Presbyterian Church, which his parents had helped to start. Church was significant to Bob, as it was to me. One day Bob drew our relationship as a triangle, with God, himself, and me as the points. Having God an important part of our love mattered to both of us, though there were times when it might have been awkward to remember. Not going all the way meant that we did everything but, and as often as we could. I masturbated quietly at night to relieve the tension, embarrassed at my urgency, keeping my breath regular so as not to disturb my roommate. Across the miles, I suspect Bob did the same.

Sometimes it seemed as if waiting to get married would be impossible. When Bob graduated from Colgate, he went to work with French's, selling mustard and spices in northern New Jersey, where he lived in a big Montclair house with a bunch of guys. I considered accelerating my course work so I could graduate early and get married sooner. Marjorie Kauffman, my English lit adviser, was unequivocal in her reaction to the idea. "Nonsense, Mary Ann!" she pronounced. "You have the rest of your life to be married. You have just these four years to be in college." I listened to her and decided to stay put, a decision that made it possible for me to savor the full banquet Mount Holyoke spread before me. It was a decision I never regretted.

The same month I graduated from Mount Holyoke, June 1960, I

turned twenty-two, and Bob and I were married. By now he had left French's, completed six months of army reserves, and was working for the Weyerhaeuser Company in Rochester, living in an apartment that would be ours when we returned from our honeymoon. We married at Brighton Presbyterian Church, with my pastor and Bob's, from Twelve Corners Presbyterian, officiating.

Ours was a traditional wedding, short and sweet. The way we saw it, the ceremony was a gate we needed to pass through to reach our goal of being married. We didn't give much thought to the ceremony; we followed the script we had heard all our lives. On our wedding weekend, Bob's parents hosted the rehearsal dinner at the University Club, my parents the reception at the American Association of University Women house.

I have three favorite pictures of our wedding day. One is of the two of us walking down the aisle together after the service. My, we were young, I think now, looking at the photo—and so pleased with ourselves. Another favorite picture is of the receiving line as Bob Hager, my brother-in-law, brings their three daughters down it. My sister Jean, matron of honor, demurely covers her cleavage with one hand while leaning down to speak to Ginny, one of the three-year-old twins, who had been scolded for trying to peek under the hoop skirt of my dress. Betsy, the other twin, is shaking hands formally with Bob, while Barbara, two years old, is skipping happily down the line with her arms out and a big smile on her face. My other favorite is our going-away photo: I'm in a blue linen dress with matching hat, and Bob is in a suit. Without his belt. I told you we were in a hurry.

After the afternoon wedding and reception, we said goodbye to family and friends and drove out of town. At last we were free, sexually, and we were thoroughly in love. We'd been Good, and now we were ready for the sweet reward of Plenty. But we were both so inexperienced at sex that to be honest, I wondered, "Is that it?" A code of inhibition had been established in our upbringing. We never got very adept at talking about our intimate desires or needs. We muddled happily along, learning from experience, and often it was fantastic.

For Bob

We round a bend in the road,
discover a scene so splendid we catch our breath.
I enjoy it because it presents an exercise in description
        and I mentally poeticize the azure sky,
            the sparkling foliage—
and you enjoy it.

We walk hand in hand on a forest path,
sunlight filtering through the pines as in a Disney film.
I enjoy it because I've brought this great book along
        so we can identify the wild flowers
        and look for maidenhair ferns—
and you enjoy it.

We sit beneath Ravinia's stars-speckled canopy,
dancers swirling on stage and fireflies glittering at the edge
    of the night.
I enjoy it because I'm following the melodic theme
        from instrument to instrument
        and picking out social satire, intended or not—
and you enjoy it.

I don't know how you got this way,
how you embrace life with such zest and naturalness
and enjoy it without description, classification,
>> analysis, or explanation,
>> but I know you do—
and I enjoy it.

Chapter 4

IN SPITE OF Mount Holyoke's vibrant academic environment, the East Coast college norm of the fifties was for most women to be married soon after graduation. Odd as it seems, given the extraordinary quality of our educations, we were willing, even eager, to trade the richness of our own intellectual exploration and expansion for the security of marriage. Love called for it; society expected it. I had no argument with this, as I had no burning sense of a career for myself and was more than ready to get married and "settle down." In more recent years, observing my daughter and daughter-in-law, both of whom had advanced degrees and careers in their fields before marriage, I marvel at my readiness to hitch my future to my husband's dreams without a clue about my own.

Ours has been called the bridge generation, between the traditionalists of the fifties and the baby boomers who instigated the volatile sixties, with a foot in both camps. I had a few friends who moved right from college into careers—but only a few. Though most of my contemporaries and I went on to careers later and had to face the fallout that changing expectations of marriage brought, most of our early marriages conformed to a traditional model (think Ward and June Cleaver). It was assumed that husbands would have careers and be the providers, that wives would stay home, raise the children, and be in charge of the social and cultural life of the family. Most of us who worked during early marriage had "until" jobs, held only until we became pregnant or "showed." I was secretary to the director of admissions at the University of Rochester, for example, a job my cousin Margie expedited from her position in the Alumni Office down the hall. "Until" jobs rarely developed into careers. Husbands' careers took precedence, determined where we lived, when we moved, and to where. A Good girl turned Good wife supported this with graciousness and charm, mindful of the Plenty that would be hers in the end. In short, we were younger versions of our parents, though of course we would do it better.

Joining the Woodruff family in marriage was an education in itself. Bob's parents were active members of Twelve Corners Presbyterian Church, having helped start it. The Woodruffs introduced me to Christmas Eve church, Twelve Corners style. The service ended at midnight and was always followed by a party given by the Woodruffs' best friends, a food and beer keg extravaganza to which the next generation, young adults by the time I joined the crowd, was cordially invited.

Eddie (Edna, though always called Eddie) and Hoke Woodruff were as different as night and day. Eddie was an entertaining extrovert who would gleefully stay up until all hours if there were someone to talk to. Hoke was a quiet lawyer who retired to bed early each evening. For all their differences, Hoke and Eddie cherished each other dearly and delighted in each other's strengths. They could have a knockdown, drag-out fight and be laughing within minutes. Bob and his sister, Ellen, always knew they were loved, unconditionally. When any Woodruff left the house, Eddie would sing out, "Be always!" The departing one would call back, "Kind!" and close the door on Eddie's final note, "And true!"

The Woodruffs' glass-half-full optimism was mystifying to me, so different from my own family's earnest cautiousness. The mantra that followed me out the Sparklin door was my father's: "Anything worth doing is worth doing well." And further: "Anything worth starting is worth finishing." I was well into adulthood before I could stop reading a book I didn't like. But I digress.

Bob and I tripped up on role expectations in early marriage. I remember being flabbergasted that he wanted to be part of decisions about decorating our apartment. As far as I knew, my father never had a thing to say about home decoration, but maybe that was because he was colorblind. On the other hand, Bob knew nothing about carving a turkey, which I considered man's work, having watched my father's surgical precision with carving knives all my life.

We expected our first baby in September 1962. It was a great expectation; it was also the natural next step for us. We lived in an apartment complex in Rochester with several other young couples, and we were all having babies. Ann and Jack Uhlir had beaten us all to the punch with their little girl. Ron and Lenore Kintisch were expecting, as were Alan and Sally Shepherd, our next-door neighbors. It was an exciting time.

When my water broke, my doctor told me to stay home until I had contractions fifteen minutes apart. I sat on towels for twenty-four hours—no contractions. The doctor, concerned about infection for the baby, told us to come to the hospital and he would induce labor. He gave me a shot. He, Bob, and I watched TV in some lounge into the night. Every so often, another shot. Finally, I was taken to the labor room, where I continued with pitocin through an IV.

The labor room had four beds. In one corner, a woman was screaming. From another corner came a voice. "This is my fourth;

it doesn't have to be like that." I lay in my corner, shaking. Nothing much was happening. Right after a nurse told me I was half-dilated, the big, bearing down contractions began. Off I went to the delivery room and very shortly our son arrived. "Will you tell Bob?" I asked the doctor. Bob was down the hall, pacing the fathers' waiting room.

"I know what," said the doctor. "Why don't you tell him yourself?" He laid our baby, wrapped and toasty, in my arms and wheeled my bed out and down the hall so Bob and I could be together. What a moment. September 12, 1962. The baby had a full head of black hair. We gave him the boy's name we'd been saving, Thomas Sparklin Woodruff. We looked at his tiny fingers, counted his toes, smiled into each other's eyes at our good fortune. After that, he was taken to the nursery, and I was wheeled to my room and slept.

Some time later that morning, someone came to my room and told me the baby was having trouble breathing. They were taking him to the preemie unit and placing him in an isolette. Most of that day and the next, Bob stood in front of the window to the preemie unit, breathing as fast as Thomas was, trying to breathe for him. Bob pushed me to the window in a wheelchair once. Our tiny boy was working so hard to make it. Bob was frantic, but I was calm. I knew Thomas would be fine.

Our sweet baby, Thomas, died the evening of his second day of life. As a violent thunderstorm burst outside, a nurse came to my room to tell me. Visiting hours had just ended. My roommate ran down the hall hoping to catch Bob, but he was gone.

I sat in my bed, battered by the thunder, flinching as rain pelted the windows. What? It couldn't be. It *couldn't* be. What? It was. What? Then out of the blue—*he wasn't baptized*. Oh, God. What would happen to him now? I fell to pieces. I rocked. I wailed.

Where did that come from? We weren't Catholic. Baptism for Presbyterians has nothing to do with getting into heaven. For us, it means welcoming a new child into the fellowship of the church—and Bob and I didn't even belong to a church at the time. My roommate, the woman who had reassured me in the labor room and who now had her fourth baby, was Catholic. "Don't worry," she said over and over. "He'll be in heaven. Don't worry."

Someone reached Bob, and he came back to the hospital. They moved us to a private room, with apologies they didn't have one other than on the maternity floor. Our obstetrician joined us. We all cried. He suggested an autopsy to determine what had happened. I'm so sorry, he said, I'm so sorry.

My parents and Bob's father arrived. No one knew what to say. My family's pastor came and suggested that we have the baby cremated, that he hold a small memorial service for immediate family right there in the hospital chapel. Then, he said, we should go on with our lives. Stunned with anguish, we agreed. The day came. Bob wheeled me to the chapel, where our parents and my sister sat, gray faced. It was all over in, maybe, five minutes. Don't ask me what the minister said; I wasn't there.

When it was time to leave the hospital, we couldn't bear to go to our apartment. We went to my parents for a week or so, then to Bob's. Bob became a brick when I fell apart. He went over to our apartment and packed away all the baby's things, knowing that I couldn't face the task. And then we went home.

Home without a baby: what to do about the milk? I'd sit in the tub, milk streaming from my breasts, tears streaming from my eyes. Allan and Sally Shepherd came home with their daughter. Their apartment happily exploded with baby things, baby noises; ours next door was so damned neat, so quiet. The Kintisches had their son. Like the Shepherds, they tiptoed around their joy in front of us, and we tried extra hard to be happy for them.

Thomas Sparklin Woodruff—I want to write his whole name again. I was afraid to suggest my maiden name again for either of our children who followed. It was as if I thought the name was spooked. Still, I'm proud to know that my firstborn son had my name in his. He represents the last generation with the name Sparklin. When someone came to my hospital room with papers identifying him as "Baby Boy Woodruff," I refused to sign them. "No!" I said, "He came into the world as Thomas Sparklin, and he will go out with his own name." The papers were reworked.

Within a month of Thomas's birth and death, Bob got a promotion. He was asked to move to the Albany area and take on the eastern New York territory. We were happy to leave Rochester, given the weight of our half-empty apartment and the wrenching adjustment we'd already had to make. We rented a house in Delmar with tufted titmice and nuthatches in the back yard, found our way to a tiny Presbyterian church that needed us, made some friends, and began to mend.

Grief is an isolating experience. Absolutely no one knows how you are feeling, no one can really understand at any one moment. Even Bob and I, though we grieved the same event, did it differently and went into that deep well at different times and in our own ways. It was often hard to even share what we were feeling with each other, because when he was up, I didn't want to bring him down, and when he was down, I had all I could do to hold the "up" energy. I went through a dreadful time of blaming myself, trying to understand what I had done to cause Thomas's death. The Plenty of parenthood wasn't to be ours, at least not yet, and that was bad, which meant I must have not been Good enough. God wasn't part of the agony or blame; it was all on me. This was the first time in my whole life when I couldn't make happen something I really, really wanted. I tortured myself over it.

We found out later, through a friend who filed the autopsy report, that our baby had had a brain hemorrhage at birth. There was nothing to suggest it would ever happen again. Gradually I began to accept that grief and unexpected loss are part of being human. Welcome to the real world, I thought. I was twenty-four and Bob was twenty-six. It was time.

Grief Is To Live With

March 1963

> Out of it all,
> a blue-cold fact
> that no confidence,
> no tears, no embrace removes:
>
> Sorrow cannot really be shared,
> be drowned in weeping,
> suffocated in doing—
> grief is to live with.
>
> Amidst the pleasant day-to-day,
> behind the deepest, fullest love,
> hidden in busy-ness—and so alone—
> grief is to live with.

Even the nearest ones cannot know,
cannot feel the quickened pulse,
weird pleasure-pain
unwelcome memory stirs.

Truth is that we cannot solve.
Off-guard, the lonely ache returns.
Cry out, "Unfair!" and yet accept.
Grief is to live with.

Midwest

Chapter 5

IN MAY 1963, we transferred to Chicago with Bob's new job at Weyerhaeuser. We arrived in the Midwest, still rocking from the death of our Thomas, and we lost a second pregnancy before we scarcely were settled. Bob's new boss and his wife took us in with open arms.

We bought a two-bedroom Cape Cod style house in Clarendon Hills, a village of six thousand people and one of a long string of contiguous suburbs that stretch westward from Chicago to Naperville along the Burlington Northern Railroad line. We joined the Community Presbyterian Church. Bob rode the Burlington eighteen miles east to Chicago for work each day. I stayed home fixing up the house, getting to know the village and our neighbors, taking my temperature, hoping to get pregnant again.

To our East Coast sensibilities, Clarendon Hills seemed to embody the very best of hometown Middle America. It was charming, classic. Fourth of July parades included all the Scouts and Little League teams, boys and girls on decorated bikes, fire engines, and Jaycee clowns, topped off with ice cream served on the village green in the center of the tiny business district. On Christmas Eve the entire community set luminarias out on the winding streets of the village to light the way for the Christ child. Bags, sand, and candles were made available behind the hardware store as a fundraiser for the Infant Welfare League.

We were thrilled—and anxious—when we knew we had another child on the way two years after the due date of our first. When our second son was born, September 18, 1964, the doctor pronounced him "a keeper." We named him James Hoke for our fathers and called him Jim. Like Thomas, Jim, too, was a little early. He was long and really skinny. His bluish skin stretched taut from bone to bone. His chin quivered when he cried. He was gorgeous. When we brought him home, it was magic. Having a new baby is like receiving the best gift in the world, one that unwraps itself a little each day. We were besotted. We could not let go of him. I nursed Jim for hours, watching him, Chicago Cubs games, and then the World Series that fall. Bob was studying for his MBA at Northwestern and did most of his reading lying on the sofa with Jim asleep on his chest. By now we had a dog, too—an unruly Lab mix we named Misty. House, baby, dog. Now we were truly a family.

Two years later, on October 16, 1966, our daughter, Katie, was born. Katie burst into the world as if she couldn't wait. Experience told us that my deliveries had a pattern: get half-dilated, then watch out! The doctor got to the hospital just in time to catch her, declaring her "a ten on the Apgar scale." We named her Katherine Ellen, Katherine because we wanted to call a little girl Katie, Ellen because it had been a name in Bob's mother's family for generations and this was Eddie Woodruff's first granddaughter. My mother quickly found a Katie in her family tree, so everyone was satisfied. Katie was compact, happy, and easy. Jim adored his baby sister, and she quickly began giggling when he came in view. All that fall, as I nursed Katie and read books to Jim, I marveled at how lucky I was. Life was truly good. Good and Plenty.

Holding An Infant

You hold an infant long before you see her.

She's in your heart when
   you first suspect
she may be on the way.

You speak to her as she flutters in your womb,
   you dream for her and
   of her as you hold
your expanding belly.

You marvel as she stretches and turns,
   an unseen miracle forming in the dark,
   getting ready for her appearance,
getting ready to make your sense of family complete.

By the time she is in your arms
   you have loved her beyond words already;
   what you hold now
     is music.

* * *

Concentrating as hard as we did to establish our family, living in a suburban setting that could have inspired a Norman Rockwell *Saturday Evening Post* cover, the upheavals of the sixties seemed removed at first. On November 22, 1963, when Walter Cronkite broke into the conversation Nancy and Grandpa were having in the kitchen on "As the World Turns," a soap opera I admit to watching, I was impatient. What did he mean, President Kennedy had been shot? And then, horrifyingly, he died. A friend called me while we were both glued to our separate TVs.

I remember crying into the phone. "This doesn't happen in America!"

"No," she sobbed, "not in our America."

But it had. And worse followed. Chicago was to be in the thick of it.

My parents were Republicans, Rockefeller Republicans, my sister and I say now, remembering the governor of our home state whose platform rested on social justice and fiscal restraint. I grew up assuming I was a Republican. My first vote in a presidential election had been a knee jerk for Nixon in 1960, the year Jack Kennedy won one of the closest presidential elections in history. In 1964, deeply influenced by Bob's boss and his wife who were conservative Republicans, I threw my support behind Barry Goldwater against Lyndon Johnson. (Didn't a Good wife vote with the husband's boss?) When I voted for George McGovern for president in 1972, signaling my forever switch to the Democratic Party, Bob recalled my vote for Goldwater eight years earlier. "Show her an idealist," he said, laughing, "and she'll vote for him." Bob was still in the Republican camp at that time, but I had begun to think for myself.

It was church that started me on that move.

Chapter 6

THE YOUNG ADULT GROUP at Community Presbyterian Church opened a coffee house, the Vine and Branch, in autumn of 1964, in a storefront on the one commercial street in Clarendon Hills. The woman who was to be program director moved away just as they were about to open. When our Jim was a couple of weeks old, the assistant pastor asked if I'd consider taking on the role of program director. I said yes. That meant that I filled the bookshelves with all the radical poetry and progressive literature I could find—Ferlinghetti, Kerouac, Ginsberg—a fun use of my Mount Holyoke English literature major. I found a play-reading group from the Hinsdale Covenant Church and scheduled musicians to perform on the tiny stage in the front window of the Vine. Before long I volunteered on staff every Sunday night, sometimes taking Jim with me in an infant seat.

The Vine and Branch's founders envisioned the coffee house as a hub for suburban twenty-somethings looking for the kind of intellectual conversation one imagined was lacking in a placid suburban setting. To our surprise, the largest group of customers turned out to be a motorcycle gang, who roared up in front of the coffee house, slung leathered legs over their steaming machines, and loped through our doors, dropping patched and studded jackets over the chairs as they settled their chains and bodies into them. We might be in the 'burbs, but the world was coming to us. It would be impossible not to get involved.

Though we either did not know it or didn't pay attention to it, the deed to the house we bought in Clarendon Hills said it could be sold only to Caucasians. Racially restrictive covenants were declared unenforceable by the US Supreme Court in 1948 (Shelley v. Kraemer), but not illegal until 1968 (Federal Fair Housing Act). Some of our neighbors had moved to Clarendon Hills to get away from Chicago neighborhoods that were becoming integrated. When Martin Luther King Jr. was assassinated in 1968, the west and south sides of Chicago erupted in riots and fire. Some of our Clarendon Hills friends had grown up on the very streets where these riots occurred. Our friend Jack Busch's father had a brick hurled through the front window of his car on Chicago's South Side. Tension was high in our village.

John David Burton was senior pastor of the Community Presbyterian Church we had joined as soon as we arrived. He ministered to his suburban flock while keeping one eye on the smoldering city to the east of us. He and his wife had nearly caused their own riot in a previous church in Mount Holly, New Jersey, when they invited a black schoolteacher, who couldn't find any place to live in their town, to stay with them. John was no stranger to racism and had no fear of challenging it. After the riots in Chicago inspired by Martin Luther King, Jr.'s killing, he and the youth fellowship leaders at Community Presbyterian arranged for the high-school youth to go into the city to tutor kids in the projects, and they put out a call for drivers. I said I'd be happy to be a driver, if they'd give me a kid, too.

I met the middle-school girl I was to tutor, and we began to work on her reading. It quickly became clear that I was the one who would learn more from our meetings. As easily as I might describe a trip to the grocery store, she would tell me of attacks she'd been subjected to on the way to or from school—guys groping her budding breasts, a girlfriend being raped while she escaped. It was only twenty-six miles from Clarendon Hills to Chicago's South Side, but it was a world away to us. I began to listen to the news with new ears. Bobby Kennedy, running for the Democratic nomination for president in 1968, spoke with passion about the rights of the poor, the lack of opportunity for them. I had my own evidence in the soft, shy voice of a twelve-year-old black girl who was up against barriers I could hardly imagine, let alone know how to overcome. Then Bobby was assassinated.

There was a war on—a messy war, Vietnam—and protestors were getting louder and more violent in their opposition. I wasn't sure how I felt about the war, but I witnessed the chaos at the Democratic National Convention in Chicago in 1968, the violent confrontation between antiwar protestors and the police. Tear gas filled the streets outside the Palmer House Hotel on Michigan Avenue, filtered across into the lakeside Grant Park where we'd gone many a midsummer's evening for concerts at the pavilion. It was a chaotic time. Hubert Humphrey won the nomination at that convention. I voted with my fear that year, voted again for Nixon, hoping he could bring some order to the chaos. In November 1969, when news of the My Lai massacre hit our television screen, I was appalled. All those women, children, and elderly people slaughtered. The cover-up, too—the massacre had been kept from the US public for a year. I began to question a war that made animals of American soldiers. In "my" war, World War II, American GIs were the good guys who saved the world from a despot and liberated Europe. But, people said, in that war the enemy was easily identifiable. In Vietnam anyone might be an enemy, so slaughter and napalming of whole villages could be justified. I was disconcerted by that rationale.

"I am the vine, you are the branches." Serving at the coffee house and tutoring with the church youth group showed me new varieties of those branches. Within me was a clear voice: "To whom much is given, of her much shall be required." I didn't know what that would mean for me, but I was awakening and looking for the invitation.

Through all of these turbulent years for the nation, our marriage was a solid foundation for our growing family. Bob and I were so very happy to be parents at last. As soon as Katie could stand, she began to toddle after her brother. They became great friends and kept us laughing with their antics. It was a joy to see the world through the eyes of our children. I packed peanut butter sandwiches, and we went to the next block to watch a steam shovel dig the basement for a new home, returning home to hot cocoa and *Mike Mulligan and Mary Ann*. We'd hike to the marshy thicket at the end of the street during the spring melt and stomp the ice into shards. We collected pussy willows and, later, pollywogs. Inside, Jim and Katie made endless blanket structures in the living room that could be Indian tents or obstacle courses, depending on the games they invented. When we got a new refrigerator, we took the carton down to the basement where they created an airplane, then a race car, entertaining themselves for days. In the backyard they hid out under the bushes or the willow tree's weeping branches, playing forts with the neighbor kids. Bob was a playful dad, involved before it was fashionable for men to be so. He wrestled with the kids. He brought the poems of A. A. Milne to life with pantomimes that sent us all into gales of laughter. Say, "Has anybody seen my mouse?" to either of our kids today, and even though they are in their forties, they will both tumble to the floor and start searching under the nearest bed.

Bob's job went well, and we both had volunteer work that mattered to us. Bob became an elder at church, a Jaycee, a leader in our small village. Besides the Vine and Branch, I volunteered in the start-up village library. When we were home, we had each other and our family. Under our roof, Good and Plenty reigned.

Helping establish the library was perhaps the most satisfying volunteer work I've ever done. It all began shortly after we moved to Clarendon Hills, when a group of women decided to build a library in town. The state of Illinois had been carved into library districts, and they discouraged these village mothers, saying our town was part of the Hinsdale library district and didn't qualify for its own. But the mothers argued that it wasn't safe for the children to have to ride their bikes across Route 83, the four-lane highway that separated Clarendon Hills from Hinsdale, to get to Hinsdale's library. They purchased a small house in the center of town just north of our village hall and put out the call to the community: clean out your bookshelves, your attics; bring your extra books to us. We're going to have a library.

I got involved with the library at that point. There was only one "real" librarian among the volunteers; the rest of us just rolled up our sleeves, decided what needed to be done, studied how to do it, and went to work. I joined the group of women who had taken on the job of sorting and cataloging books, and loved both the work and the women I met. They were bright, well read, interesting. It made my days to work with them. Once we had the library up and running and people were using it regularly, we went to the village and asked for tax money to build the collection. The village reacted enthusiastically. Now that we were tax supported, our committee became the book selection and cataloguing committee. And now we needed an official library board. I was elected as one of its members. All went so well that we began to outgrow our space.

We went back to the village and got approval for a new building. We hired an architect whose plans we liked. In a marathon effort, volunteers packed the library, using any boxes we could get from local merchants. (It was months before some sections of the reestablished library stopped smelling of fish or onions!) Then the call went out for help, and one Saturday all the Boy Scouts, Cub Scouts, Girl Scouts, and Brownies in town, all the Little League teams and their parents—the whole village, it seemed—arrived and set up a firefighter's carry line from the little house to the basement of the village hall next door. We moved the entire library by hand in one day, and within a week, the temporary library was open for business. Then we razed the original house and built a brand-new library building on that property.

Again we packed up the library collection. Again the village arrived en masse to help pass the cartons hand-to-hand from the village hall basement to the new building. Senator Charles Percy (R–Illinois) came for the grand opening, dedicating the library to the volunteers who had made it a reality, which meant nearly every single person in the village. It was a marvelous event.

Bob and I developed lifelong friends in Clarendon Hills. My women friends helped each other figure out when the kids needed stitches, talked over coffee while our kids played together, took up bridge and tennis. As couples, we danced and got into devilment together on weekends. We played broom hockey on the frozen village pond in winter and created elaborate treasure hunts for a gang of dozens in summer.

A part of the sixties that didn't register much with me was feminism. Betty Friedan's *The Feminine Mystique* was getting a lot of press, but not where I lived. Eddie Woodruff knew someone who knew

Betty Friedan and reported that her house was a pigsty. To Eddie, this negated anything she might have written about the place of women. Eddie's judgment was so commanding, I was intimidated. *The Feminine Mystique* came into the library, but not to our house.

I never read Friedan. Yet somewhere in the sixties I read the book *Mrs. Beneker* by Violet Weingarten. In one scene, Mrs. Beneker visits her doctor. "I have a wonderful husband and two great children," she tells the doctor. "Why am I not happy?" That piece of Mrs. Beneker's story disturbed me deeply, haunted me, but I could not have begun to tell you why.

John Burton, the senior pastor of our church, became a special friend of mine during these years. His was a powerful presence, a dark and brooding nature. Our friendship was woven from strands of church responsibility and shared pain for the world. He and I anchored the Sunday night shift at the Vine and Branch with two others. We danced together at parties. John often dropped in for coffee, chatting for a few minutes while the children played at our feet. He and Katie had a special bond from the moment she ran to him in the hallway of the church the first time I delivered Jim to preschool. John answered something in me: a yearning for depth, a willingness to look at the darker side of life.

In the late sixties, some people we knew were coming back from vacations at Esalen at Big Sur, California, talking of hot tubs and encounter groups. To a person, they said their experiences at Esalen were incredible, powerful, but they found it nearly impossible to put them into words. We did hear names like Fritz Perls, Carl Rogers, Jean Houston, and George Leonard, and of course we were curious. John Burton and a few others decided to bring some of the movers and shakers of this new human potential movement to the Midwest.

When Jack Gibb, a wonderful man, came to town, Bob and I and probably fifty others attended his TORI Community weekend. TORI stood for trusting, opening, realizing, and interdepending. Under his leadership we had a group experience that brought all of us closer together and made us more open than we had been before as social friends. John Burton and I did the blind trust walk together.

Shortly after the TORI Community weekend, John observed over coffee one morning that while I was very warm with him, there was always some reserve, something I held back. I said, "Of course I hold back; I can imagine what might happen if I didn't."

He threw back his head and laughed. "You've thought of it, too!" he said with delight. We sat quietly across from each other, absorbing this new information. The coffee in my mug grew cool. I knew we were special friends. I knew I was flattered by his attention, that he met something in me I obviously wanted met. But I was not prepared to take it further. Neither, once the possibility had been voiced, was he. Reason spoke next. We knew that our friendship depended on the trust of Bob Woodruff and Jean Burton, and there was no way we would violate that trust or do something sure to ruin the friendship.

We both were writing poetry in those days, sometimes finishing each other's stanzas. Poetry had seemed like a safe container for the attraction, but now I wasn't so sure. That was the poetry I later burned. John published many of his in a book he titled *Naked in the Street*.

Once Katie entered kindergarten, I knew it was time to pull the plug on my coffeepot and make myself less available. Volunteering in the village library had been so captivating that I decided I was meant to be a librarian. It was the first notion I ever had of a career, and it felt like time to get moving on it. I enrolled part time in library school at Rosary College in Oak Park and squeezed in classes during the time

Katie was in school.

We lived in the Midwest for ten years. In early 1973, Jim and Katie were in third and first grade, I had started my third course in library school, and we had moved to our dream home in the village. Bob came home from a trip with the news that he was being promoted. His new job would be at Weyerhaeuser headquarters in Tacoma, Washington.

Pacific Northwest

Chapter 7

BOB AND I TRAVELED to the Pacific Northwest for a house-hunting trip in February 1973. Weyerhaeuser's headquarters was located halfway between Seattle and Tacoma. We decided we'd look near Seattle for a house. That way we could steer clear of Weyerhaeuser politics (more Weyerhaeuser people lived in Tacoma or Lakewood, south of Tacoma, than in Seattle), and I could easily continue library school at the University of Washington. A billboard in Seattle read, "Would the last person leaving Seattle turn out the lights?" pointing out that we were arriving in the Northwest in the midst of what came to be known as the Boeing Bust. The SST had been cancelled by the federal government; that and changing demand for aircraft resulted in nearly 44 percent of the employees of Seattle's major corporation losing their jobs. The slump lasted until the mid eighties, although the relocation of Microsoft in 1979 from Albuquerque to Redmond, east of Lake Washington, ensured that Seattle was never again a "one-horse" town.

We were house hunting the week when all the schools in the region were voting on levies, and we paid attention. Searching areas that historically passed school levies led us to Mercer Island and Bellevue. We chose a house on Mercer Island, because it reminded us of Glen Lake, Michigan, where we had rented a cabin every summer vacation for five years. (We had watched Neil Armstrong's first step onto the moon from a portable television on Glen Lake's beach the night of July 20, 1969.) We were drawn to Mercer Island's clear, clean air, tall trees, lack of sidewalks, and view of Lake Washington through the trees.

In April, we piled the kids and our miniature schnauzer in the back of Miss Piggy, our blue station wagon, loaded the middle seats with houseplants, and drove out of our driveway in Illinois. We were waved off by the good friends who'd come to help us clean the house and say good-bye. My friends and I had cried for weeks. I was heartsick that we were leaving this place that meant so much to us. I knew there would never be friends like these, never be a church like ours. I would never walk into a drugstore again and have the druggist sing out, "Hi, Mrs. Woodruff!" Poor Bob.

Miss Piggy lumbered across the prairie, through the Badlands, past Mount Rushmore, over the Grand Tetons, and across the Continental Divide. We followed the Lewis and Clark Trail part of the way, stopping at Register Rock where covered wagon train members had scratched their names as they made the crossing to the West. I felt as if our journey was as monumental as theirs. Completing the drive across Washington State, we took Jim and Katie's pictures by a sign that read, Welcome to Mercer Island. The moving van arrived the next day, and so did the Welcome Wagon lady. It was pouring rain.

The point of moving in April was so our kids could settle into school and make some friends before summer. They loved the walk to school through the fir, hemlock, and alder ravine between our neighborhood and Island Park School. "It's like a jungle!" Jim exclaimed, wide-eyed. In May, the school community had its end-of-year ice-cream social, and Bob and I were excited to go. We wanted to make some friends, too. I showered and put on a clean shirt and slacks for the occasion, and Bob changed after work to casual clothes. This would have been standard attire for an ice-cream social in Clarendon Hills, but when we got to Island Park School that night it seemed to us that everyone else was dressed for a cocktail party. What have we gotten into? we asked ourselves when we got home. Where will we find our friends?

We spent that summer doing every Seattle thing we could think of to do, exploring our new territory. When Bob looked at me one night and said, "You're really having fun, aren't you?" I was chagrined. I think he was afraid I would never get over leaving Illinois. I've learned I always grieve in the face of endings, that letting go has always been difficult for me—heck, I can hardly throw out a dead houseplant. But I've also discovered I'm seldom homesick once I've moved to a new space, and that certainly was true for the Pacific Northwest. What's tough is that I seldom remember this pattern from one dislocation to the next.

By the fall of our first year, we had joined Mercer Island Presbyterian Church and had begun to make a group of friends. All transplants from other places, we say even now that we chose each other as friends so we would have aunties and uncles for our kids. These families introduced us to the best of Pacific Northwest outdoor life: hiking, camping, backpacking, boating, water skiing, biking. And food: mussels, salmon, Dungeness crab. We did most everything as families, our kids entering in and enjoying it all right along with us. This was new for us, and we loved it. Within a few years, six families, including ours, began going to Fort Worden, a former military post turned state park on the Olympic Peninsula, for Thanksgiving weekend. This is a tradition we've kept up to this day; now the aunties and uncles are grandparents to a whole new generation, as our kids return with their kids for the annual get-together.

The Pacific Northwest has the lowest rate of church attendance in the United States. This may be because of the spectacular outdoor activities competing for one's weekend time. Church commitment is a conscious choice, not a habit, which made a qualitative difference to our experience of church. Mercer Island Presbyterian (MIPC) grounded us and our young family, gave us a home away from home, provided structure, inspiration, intellectual challenge, a place to flex our leadership muscles, a community of common values, and safe mentoring for our children during their growing-up years. My closest women friends, a group of eight of us "chosen sisters" who have traveled together, laughed, cried, and supported each other through nearly forty years of everything life can throw at us, came together through MIPC.

The church also took me to my first women's retreat, that first fall of 1973. In a ramshackle Bible camp on Lake Sammamish east of Lake Washington, I was introduced to the idea of women's small groups—women studying, praying together, and supporting each other. I came home with a growing sense of belonging and a glimmer of connecting to God at a deeper and more personal level than I had ever known before. I joined one of the new small groups and dove into Bible study, prayer, and intimate sharing with my new friends.

It constantly amazed me that we were living in a landscape we had only seen previously in Marlboro commercials. Our first New Year's Day in the Pacific Northwest, we drove an hour to the Cascade Mountains east of us to play in the snow with friends who were at Snoqualmie Pass for a ski weekend. We drove back home observing sailboats on Lake Washington, and in our backyard, roses were still in bloom. "You wouldn't believe this," I wrote to my parents.

The following August we traveled the Oregon coast. We camped a couple of nights at Oswald West State Park, a no-vehicle park on a cove sheltered between two coastal headlands. We carried our tent, stove, and belongings in a wheelbarrow from the parking lot down through a forest of Sitka spruce to our campsite. After dinner we played Frisbee on the cove's broad beach until twilight, and then by the light of our Coleman lantern until dark somewhere around ten o'clock—one of the pleasures of the long summer evenings in the Pacific Northwest. When we turned in, lights from native fishing boats twinkled through the night at the outer entrance to the cove. The second evening, August 9, we joined our fellow campers trekking back up the path to the parking lot, where we all sat in our cars and listened to President Nixon resign from office. I may have been the last person to hold out hope that the president had not been involved in the Watergate scandal. Still, it was a very quiet group that trouped back to camp, most of us shaking our heads in stunned silence.

Bob's new job required a lot of travel, much of it international. He brought the world to our dinner table with stories and with guests who were his customers or translators from Europe and Japan. I held down the home front while completing my library degree at the University of Washington and serving on the long-range planning committee at church, where Bob and I taught fifth-grade Sunday school. Jim and Katie were making their ways in the world, each finding their own rhythms, strengths, and friends.

Life was robust for us. But change was on the way. As before, it was church that started me on the move.

Chapter 8

I DIDN'T INTEND to become a consultant. It all started when I was asked to serve on the long-range planning committee at Mercer Island Presbyterian Church shortly after we joined in 1973. Riley Jensen, our new young pastor, had accepted the call to the church with the understanding that one of his first actions would be to lead the church through a planning process. While we were getting organized, Riley and I attended a Seattle presbytery workshop where Ed Lindaman, president of Whitworth College, a Presbyterian school in Spokane, presented a unique approach to long-range planning. He called it "Future Before You Plan," after a small book he had co-authored. Lindaman suggested that we involve the whole church in looking at where we thought the world would be in five to ten years and what the world might be needing from a church such as ours, given that future vision. With a strong collective sense of the church we wanted to be in the future, our strategies and action plans could follow.

We took Dr. Lindaman's approach and led our church in a participative process that was unique for the times. Everyone was involved. It was exciting, challenging, and fun. It was so successful that when the plan was followed by a request to expand the church facility to meet the vision we had created together, the design and budget passed on the first vote. I got to serve on the building committee and shortly after that was ordained as an elder and became chair of the first-ever long-range planning committee, charged with keeping the vision in front of the congregation. When other churches, hearing of our success, wanted help starting their own long-range plans, I was often called on to meet with them, opportunities I loved.

Dick Chappelle, who had chaired the long-range planning committee at MIPC, came to me in fall of 1976 with a proposition. "I need an associate in my consulting practice," he said, "and I want you."

I had just completed my masters in librarianship. "I can't do that, Dick," I demurred. "I'm going to be a librarian."

"Do you have a job yet?"

"No," I said. "I'm working on it."

"Well, if you don't, I do, and I think you can do it," insisted Dick. He explained that he had a stack of resumes from which he needed someone to cull five or six for phone interviews. Well, I could do that, I thought. So I did. When that job was finished, Dick had another proposition. This time he wanted me to help him interview employees at a firm where conflict was rife. Well, I thought, I could do that. So I did. Soon I was dressing in my business "costume" and meeting Dick downtown for work parts of several days a week. I felt like I was playacting. I read a lot, studying to stay a page ahead of our clients, hoping no one would discover I was a fraud. As a mentor, Dick had confidence for both of us.

When Dick left his firm to join another, I went with him, as we were more or less attached at the hips by then. A year later one of his clients hired him away from that consulting firm. I stayed behind. The head of the firm assumed I was a real consultant and continued to give me assignments, some of which I really had no business doing. In 1980 I had a crisis of conscience, resigned from that firm, and went home to think. If I have any credibility in this pursuit, I said to myself, it's with the people side of consulting. I had designed some performance planning and appraisal programs that worked well, and I enjoyed the training and implementation process. I liked the part-time schedule I had, too, combining work with all school vacations off.

A friend introduced me to Donworth-Taylor, a management consulting firm specializing in compensation and labor issues. Carey Donworth and Bill Taylor were among the most respected men in Seattle. When Bill offered me a job, I was thrilled. At Donworth-Taylor I moved from performance appraisal to supervisory skills training to team building to conflict resolution, studying all the time. I took consulting skills and participative leadership skills workshops from Don Swartz, one of the deans of organization development in the region. Don then introduced me to Organization Systems Renewal (OSR), a masters program he had started. Donworth-Taylor supported me when I entered the program at Antioch University, Seattle, in 1984, the same year Katie left for college. I could use what I learned in OSR immediately, both with clients and as the author of *The Executive Report*, a bi-monthly publication we distributed to clients and friends of the firm. Gradually, Bill Taylor and I came to anchor a growing practice in participative leadership, helping clients who were interested in quality circles and other ways to involve employees at every level in making improvements in their processes.

Here's where serendipity intersects my career path. When I began the OSR program, one of the first visiting faculty who taught us was Ron Lippitt, a University of Michigan professor and consultant who ran the Institute for Social Research at Ann Arbor. Right away, he began talking about a book, *Future Before You Plan*, he had written with Ed Lindaman. Ed Lindaman! I'd met the man more than ten years earlier as president of a small northwest Presbyterian College. Now I discovered he'd been the former program director for the Apollo program at Rockwell and a renowned futurist.

Through OSR, my consulting practice soon moved in the direction of organization development (OD.) It didn't surprise me that I was good at reading people or understanding the nuanced energy in a room—that was a legacy from my childhood. Now I had a theory base to undergird it, plus new implementation skills. Dick Chappelle had taught me how to write a good consultant's report: our findings, our conclusions, our recommendations. In OSR, I learned how much more powerful it could be to facilitate clients to arrive at their own findings and conclusions and to develop their own action plans for change. It reminded me of the success of our church's long-range planning process. There's a lot more energy and commitment in creating a compelling vision of the future you want and working to make it a reality than there is in listing all the problems you have and trying to plan your way out of trouble. As I honed my skills for participative processes, I was gaining clients of my own. I liked it.

I was also maturing in other ways. A good friend from OSR had been a conscientious objector during the Vietnam War. Jay thought—rightly—that I was clueless about the complexities of the Vietnam conflict. In 1987, he took me to see the movie *Platoon*, to help me understand the way he saw the war. After the movie we went for a beer and talked for hours. I felt ill, as images played over in my head. I am still haunted when I hear Barber's *Adagio for Strings*, the film's accompaniment to new recruits jumping from the gaping maw of a military transport plane into the dusty air of "Nam" and staring at rows of body bags ready to be loaded for the return trip, a Zippo lighting the first thatch on a Vietnamese village torched by our soldiers, the same soldiers cradling the children they carry out of that village as it explodes behind them, a helicopter gliding over a burned-out valley and a crater strewn with dead bodies—American bodies, killed by American firepower. The conversation with Jay made me think of the summer of 1967, when Bob took a business seminar at the University of Wisconsin. We were living in Illinois at the time. We drove around the campus at Madison marveling at how beautiful it was, but we were shocked to see "Down With Dow!" splashed in white paint over many of the university buildings. Student protests over Dow Chemical's production of the napalm used in Vietnam had resulted in near riots when Dow recruiters visited the Wisconsin campus in February of that year. In Clarendon Hills, where we lived, most people thought the students were nut cases. The evening with Jay reminded me as well of the headlines of May 4, 1970, screaming that the National Guard had gunned down Kent State students protesting the US invasion of Cambodia. This was big news at our house—because Bob's aunt and uncle, who lived in Kent, were inconvenienced for days while tanks were parked at the end of their street by the university entrance. Now I've heard the story from my friend Stephanie, who was a student among the protestors at Kent State that day, and it's a story lodged in the pit of my stomach. Then it all seemed perplexing; it was easier to just get on with things and not think too much about it. That is part of the ease of Plenty, isn't it? It is possible not to look at things that make you uncomfortable. It took making friends with African Americans to help me understand not just plenty but privilege, white privilege—but that's another story. Suffice it to say that the night Jay introduced me to *Platoon* I was stunned as I began to realize the implications of all that had gone on while I was raising my young family in the suburbs, pretty much oblivious or otherwise occupied with my own life.

And now my own life was generating a war of sorts, a battle for change, one in which conscientious objection would not be a good option for anyone.

Bob was wholeheartedly enthusiastic about my going to work. He was my biggest fan—as long as nothing changed in his life. This worked well while I was plodding along at a part-time pace. But as I began to get more serious about having a career, and especially when I started graduate school, things at home began to be stressed. We've never forgotten the nightmare of a dinner at the Velvet Turtle when I asked Bob for some help at home. "Something has to change," I started, "I need you to do more around the house. I can't do it all any longer."

Bob blinked at me in disbelief. "No way!" he exclaimed.

"What do you mean, 'No way'?" I shot back. "You're as responsible for our house as I am."

Things quickly escalated to an appalling pitch. The wait staff would arrive in our vicinity and kind of back toward our table, extending our plates behind them and then making hasty retreats. We got nowhere with this debate. It was a silent, furious ride home.

The kids got it that roles were changing. Our college-age Jim complained one summer that he didn't understand why he always had to cut the grass. I offered to switch with him—laundry for lawn—and he accepted. Katie and her dad adored one another, and they share the Woodruff ability to state unequivocally what is on their minds. One night she observed, "Dad, just because you have a dick, you think you're the boss of everything."

I was trying to drag Bob out of the fifties into a eighties-style marriage, and he wasn't having any of it. I wasn't tactful in this. Feminism was on the rise throughout the country, and it was beginning to resonate with me. Phyllis Schlafly opposed the Equal Rights Amendment to the Constitution, but I was all for it. When Bob pointed out that he had left a shirt with a lost collar button on the bedroom doorknob for weeks, and it still hadn't been fixed, I told him that he had as much time as I had to sew on the damn button.

Breaking Out

business

MARY ANN WOODRUFF

Woodruff joins Donworth, Taylor

Mary Ann Woodruff has joined the Seattle management consulting firm of Donworth, Taylor & Co.

A Mercer Island resident, she has worked in corporate and public sector strategic planning and management development. She holds a bachelor's degree from Mount Holyoke College and a master's in library science from the University of Washington.

The Mercer Island resident is an elder of the Presbyterian Church and a charter member of the City Club.

THE FIFTH EDITION, *Mercer Island Reporter*,
Friday October 30, 1981

Chapter 9

IN 1987, Donworth-Taylor's partners asked me to become one of them. My ego sang at the possibility. I would be the only woman partner in the firm; I could imagine the fun of dropping that news at some dinner party. Then I looked more closely at the partners. Most of them worked sixty- to seventy-hour weeks. They laughed about how long it had been since they'd had a weekend with their families. I couldn't quite accept that idea for myself. I had always had a reduced schedule, starting while the children were in school. I had never wanted to become so absorbed in work that I'd lose sight of my family. One of the partners said to me, "Mary Ann, we know you have this thing about valuing time with your family. Shit, we all do. But we'd expect a partner to make the same kinds of sacrifices we're making."

There has to be another definition of success, I thought.

I went to see Alene Moris, a career and life counselor in Seattle. "What's wrong with me?" I asked, describing how the offer of partnership made my stomach cramp.

"Absolutely nothing," replied Alene. "Women have begged to have a bigger piece of the pie for years and are only now finding out that the pie makes you sick."

Alene invited me to her home the following Thursday evening where I met a group of women who were all asking the same kinds of questions: how to be successful in roles of responsibility or leadership and honor their own "feminine" sensitivities in work cultures so dominated by "masculine" values. Out of that evening came a retreat put together by all of us around Alene's table so we could have more time and involve more like-minded women in exploring these issues.

That retreat, in June 1987, was stunning for me. I'd been so busy trying to do good work, take care of my family and friends, be the good churchwoman (whatever that was), I hadn't looked up in a long time. Or out. Here in the circle of what we called the Gathering of Women were women of varied ages, backgrounds, and professions. It was an eclectic mix I would never have found on Mercer Island. The unifying factors were intelligence, an assumption of having done serious self-reflection, a willingness to share personally, and a feminist perspective that I could only honestly claim as growing in me at the time. The conversations at the Gathering were far ranging, values laden. I hadn't been so moved or laughed so hard for a long time. I felt lucky to be there, a feeling that has never left me. It is a joy to say that the Gathering of Women has retreated together every June since 1987.

I think of the Gathering as my "pod." Some of the women I see often, others only at this annual get together or on special occasions when we swim up from the various depths and shoals we inhabit to join together. By now there are more than forty women on the Gathering roster, although the annual retreat usually finds thirty-some in the circle. Some members have moved away and only come back occasionally. All have become dear friends and crucial in my life.

With the support of the Gathering and several come-to-Jesus confrontations with myself over what matters, I left Donworth-Taylor in June 1988 to start my own consulting firm. Woodruff Associates was my fiftieth birthday gift to myself. At a family party celebrating Katie's graduation from Brown and my birthday, Bob gave me a plaque with a photo of me at the helm of a sailboat. The plaque read: "To the good ship JOHN WALTER as it starts its second half century sailing new and uncharted waters. Best wishes." The plaque was a nod to my parents' early imagining that I would be a son. My parents were delighted and joined Bob on my board of directors. It was such fun having an annual board meeting with my parents. They would come to Seattle for a summer visit, and sooner or later there'd be the right night for the four of us to go to dinner, which Woodruff Associates paid for, and at which I presented the financial results of my year. Mother, my brilliant mother who I swear was born thirty years too soon, was mystified at the very idea that I had my own business. "I still don't know what you do," she declared once, shaking her head, "or how you have the nerve to do it."

Being on my own was exhilarating—and a bit scary. It took two years for me to relax into knowing that if there was a hole in my calendar, more work would come. I am forever grateful to Kathie Dannemiller, to whom Bob introduced me when she was consulting for Weyerhaeuser. Kathie (another colleague of Ron Lippitt, another Ann Arbor influence) took me under her wing, as she had many others. She was one of the gurus of large-scale systems change and she mentored me, starting with a culture change engagement for Seattle/King County Metro in the early nineties.

Metro had been established in 1958 to clean up Lake Washington. So successful was Metro at improving water quality that, in 1972, voters gave it authority to include a regional transit system in its mission. In the late eighties, the expanded water quality and transit organization conducted a survey in which the employees described Metro's culture as militaristic, racist, sexist, and homophobic.

Metro's leaders were aghast and vowed to engage the whole organization in a sincere effort to change. When I was approached by Metro asking if I was interested in the work, I asked Kathie Dannemiller to be my partner in the proposal. Kathie's personality, approach, and experience wowed Metro's executives. She, others from her firm, and I then comprised the team leading a culture change effort within Metro that involved all four to five thousand of its employees, lasted for several years, and gave me skills in working with a whole organizational system that became a hallmark of my future work.

Seattle has a flourishing organization development community. OD consultants work together when it makes sense, refer work to each other that fits with each person's gifts and interests, and mentor others as they come into the profession. Bob and I, along with an OSR friend and some other colleagues who had moved to Seattle from Ann Arbor, started the Northwest Cluster in June of 1989. We modeled the Cluster after the Lippitt Cluster in Ann Arbor. Kathie Dannemiller, a founding member of the Lippitt Cluster, was in town and joined us for the kickoff. The Cluster met monthly at our home for potluck dinner and a wide-ranging group OD conversation, the purpose of which was shared learning and growth. Anyone could attend; often there were as many as fifty persons separated into smaller clusters that met in every room in our house.

Bob, who had enjoyed what I studied as much as I did, enrolled in the OSR cohort following mine at Antioch and had his own masters in organization systems renewal by the time I established Woodruff Associates. One evening, I'm guessing in 1990, he burst in from work, brimming with exuberance. "I've got it!" he beamed. "I'm going to find a job as an internal OD consultant for Weyerhaeuser, and in a few years I'll take early retirement and join Woodruff Associates!"

I was standing in the kitchen when he exploded this idea between us. I had an instant reaction from the depths of my soul, an instant taste of something metallic in my mouth. I stared at him, thinking: NO!

Consulting was my "room of one's own." It was the first place in my adult life where I showed up as me, not as Bob's wife or Jim or Katie's mother. It was heady discovering I was good at this, that when I walked into a room as a consultant, people trusted that I had the skills they needed. I had a newfound sense of my own influence, and I didn't want to give it up to satisfy Bob's dream. If we went out into the world as co-consultants, I was sure everyone would assume he was the president and I the secretary. I was having a hard enough time trying to shift us to a new paradigm of partnership at home. How could I even begin to consider bringing that battle into a client's space? No, I said, and I meant it. At that moment, I couldn't be the Good wife. I believed that if I didn't choose myself, I would lose my soul.

You can imagine that this was not well received. Bob was hurt and disappointed. He went on with his plans, perhaps thinking I would change my mind in the end. I went on with mine, too. By this time, both Jim and Katie had graduated from college and were launched on their own, so I dug more deeply into my own craft.

Solo Song

> We all played violin in second grade,
> training in the string ensemble
> for whatever we would play in the full orchestra,
> the pride of Indian Landing school.

When they discovered I had perfect pitch
I was asked to come early
to help the teacher tune the violins.
The metaphor escaped me then
but what I did was give others voice,
a perfectly pitched voice at that.

Oh, I played my instrument too,
second violin,
but my real contribution was in that before-school
work of plunking and twisting,
enabling others to make music.

Now I continue to plunk and twist
early in the morning
so that others may have voice,
and a well-tuned voice at that.
It's what I do professionally.

But every now and then
the rebel in me wants to simply
grab an instrument,
head for the hills and play my own song,
perfectly pitched or not.

Chapter 10

BEING ON MY OWN as a consultant, I wanted to be sure my own emotional pipes were clean so that I wasn't projecting unresolved issues on clients as I worked more deeply in their organizations. I asked some colleagues I respected to suggest programs I might find helpful in this pursuit. The suggestion that kept coming up was the WeirLab in Self Differentiation. It was a ten-day residential lab led by John and Joyce Weir each August at Kirkridge, a retreat center in the Pocono Mountains of eastern Pennsylvania.

When I told Bob I wanted to do this lab in August 1989, his immediate response was, "Sounds like fun! I'll go, too!" I resisted, admitting that part of what I needed to self-differentiate from was him. He was puzzled by this, but insistent. We compromised by going together and rooming together, but sitting separately throughout the public parts of the lab. The way the lab was designed, I doubt that many people ever guessed we were married.

The WeirLab was a sonic boom in the midst of my very being. Jungian based, the WeirLab provided every possible means to become aware of one's feelings and encounter new parts of oneself, all in service of moving each of us to overcome our fears and live from a place of personal authority. Those ten days rattled every feeling and shook loose every emotion in me. The lab broke me open and plunged me into an interior terrain that changed everything. I got in touch with how profoundly terrified I had been all my life. I also found a determined Samurai warrior inside who resolved to find out why.

Two months after the WeirLab, my father became very ill and had emergency surgery for what turned out to be colon cancer. The surgery didn't go well, and he landed in the critical care unit of Strong Memorial Hospital, where he stayed for months. My sister, Jean, who was living in Connecticut, and I began trading weeks in Rochester to see our parents through the crisis. Now all my family issues were right in front of me, and now I had different lenses through which to process them.

I also had a new partner in processing my awakenings. A dark-eyed raven of a woman I'll call Rachel. She lived in Maine, a world away in every sense from me. We continued the conversations we had begun at the WeirLab—lengthy phone calls, fat letters flying coast to coast packed with observations, reflections, and feelings. Rachel was a good listener; she gave me helpful feedback on what I said or wrote, and she shared her own journey freely. The intensity and quality of our friendship filled a part of me that had been empty. She introduced me to Riane Eisler's *The Chalice and the Blade*, a book that upended my traditional religious belief system. Learning that the Judeo-Christian tradition in which I was steeped was guided in part by a patriarchal determination to undermine and displace the influence of women and the spirituality of earlier matriarchal cultures shook me to the core. I delved more deeply into spirituality and religion, especially from a feminist perspective.

In February 1990, while Bob took my turn being with Mother and helping her to get to and from the hospital through Rochester's snows to visit my father, I traveled to Boston, this time to attend a

Women's WeirLab. Rachel was my roommate at the lab. Another sonic boom. One of the leaders suggested I personify the terror I experienced. What a difference it made when I changed the word from "terror" to "terrorist." I could see the terrorist parts of me, plural because there was such a group of them. I saw them as young men in battle fatigues who carried Uzi rifles, wiry men with athletic bodies, who were hypervigilant—and had short fuses. The Samurai warrior in me said it was time to confront these terrorists.

Returning to Seattle, I found a Jungian counselor, with whom I began what would be a seven-year exploration. "I have three issues," I said to Susan the first day, cradling in shaking hands the mug of tea she'd offered. "I have this feeling as though terrorists are stalking me, ready to throw buckets of cold slop over me without any warning. My father is dying of cancer. And…I think I might be falling in love with a woman."

Chapter 11

I DIDN'T KNOW what to do with the Rachel part of me. I realized that her role in whatever discoveries I was making about myself was profound. I knew she was answering an unspoken yearning in me. Was this love? Or was I simply drawn to having someone who heard me? Fortunately, Rachel was on the East Coast. She could continue to be my WeirLab processing buddy for the time being. She was the least of my worries at the moment. I needed to do battle with the terrorists.

My understanding of Jungian concepts was fairly simple at this point. I knew we have within us both *ego* and *self*. I knew we develop a *persona* early on in our life; this is the face we present to the world, designed to keep us safe. I knew that in Jungian parlance *ego* contains what we know and *self* is home to the unconscious. Some say Jung used *self, soul,* and *God* interchangeably. I'd been told that the veil between ego and self is pretty much opaque, but that at some point, usually about midlife, previously unknown parts of the self begin to seep through the veil into conscious awareness. These parts are often unwelcome, because we've denied them, if we've had any glimpse of them before. A simple example: Suppose it occurs to me that I have a selfish part to me. I'd rather do something I want to do than be good (as the crowd defines good) and do something else. Once I'm aware, I have a choice: deny my selfishness or accept it. If I deny that I have a selfish part to me, I will stuff it back behind the veil into my unconscious. Then, chances are, I will scapegoat others for this failing. "Just look at Jenny," I might think to myself. "What a selfish bitch she is." If I can accept the selfish part of me, my inner dialogue might go something like this: "Yes, I certainly have a selfish part to me. I will own that I do. And I can choose when and when not to act on it." This would be integration, according to Jung. Jung argued that individuation is an important psychological process of integrating the unconscious with the conscious, which requires making the veil between ego and self as permeable as possible.

As a Jungian counselor, Susan emphasized the creative process to help people achieve this integration. She used dreams, images, art, photography, writing, sand tray—anything that tapped the creative energy of her clients. One day she invited me to select from the many, many small items she had on her shelves and place them in her sand tray—a shallow pan, two feet by three. Without much thought I took some objects and placed them randomly in the tray. It didn't take long to see that I had organized my family there in the sand and had even portrayed the unique character of each person.

Susan introduced me to voice dialogue, a technique through which I could speak to these newly named parts of myself. I began walking the woods near my home every morning, carrying on lengthy conversations with the terrorists. Soon other previously unknown parts began joining in our walks. I discovered a Queen of Hearts part of me. Not the demure queen who made some tarts, this was the shrew from *Alice's Adventures in Wonderland*, the one who glared at me and thrust her finger in my face, bawling, "Off with her head!" whenever she got the whim to do so. I walked and walked those woods, coming home to write pages and pages of voice dialogue in my journal. Then, on weekday mornings, I would shower, put on my business clothes, and go off to be a consultant. The challenge of my work required me to compartmentalize, and I did.

Susan also asked me to pay attention to my dreams. In one dream, I was a teacher. When I asked all the children to go outside for recess, a little black girl stayed behind. I pressed her to go play with the other kids. She looked up at me and declared, "But I just want to be with *you*." I woke up puzzled. Susan suggested I take the little black girl on my walks in the woods. I did. Often I could swear I felt her little hand in mine.

In another dream, a recurring nightmare, I'd be in the car running errands. As I returned home I would remember with a start—the baby! I'd forgotten that I left the baby at home, and I'd been gone too long. When I walked in the front door, the baby would be at the top of the stairs, sobbing with despair and exhaustion, her diaper soiled, her face smeared with snot. She had climbed out of her crib searching for me, but I had abandoned her.

Having had his own WeirLab experience, Bob was beginning to do his own work. But it hurt him when on Saturday mornings, he wanted to join me on my walks, and I said I wanted to go alone. I needed my own space, and that was hard on him.

Back in Rochester, my father continued his downward slide. He died in February 1991. Mother immediately announced to Jean and me that she would go as soon as she could into the Rochester Friendly Home, the nearby rambling brick campus where we had caroled when we were Girl Scouts. Jean and I took the liberty of going out to the home to check out availability, and we were dismayed at the shabby one-room accommodations we were shown. When we talked to Mother about this, she became livid; we had taken her power away from her. She was right. Nothing we could do would make things better.

After Jean left town, but while I was still in Rochester, I suggested to Mother that we go look at a relatively new apartment building for retirees on East Avenue. She would have none of it. I did get her into the car, but when we pulled up to the apartment building, Mother turned to me and announced, "This is all your idea, you just go in there yourself."

"Get out of the car," I retorted. "I'm only here for a few more days. Humor me." We walked into the lobby of the building. It was sunny and pleasant.

When a woman approached and greeted us, my mother glowered. "Talk to her," she snapped, gesturing toward me. "She's the one who's interested." The woman led us into her office and, smooth as could be, directed all her conversation to me. Only gradually did she begin to include Mother in her gaze. By the time we were looking at one- and two-bedroom apartments, Mother was entering into the conversation, and later she allowed as how it was an "OK place." Jean and I shared a huge sigh of relief when I described the visit to her.

Rochester had an ice storm in March that year that marooned Mother in her home without power for days. Immediately afterward, she went on a tear to move out of the house and into the apartment on East Avenue. She completed that move in early June. Interestingly, her new home was right across the street from the first apartment that she, Daddy, and Jean lived in when moving to Rochester more than fifty-five years earlier. A week after she settled in, Mother didn't disable the morning alarm by her front door. When officials broke into her apartment, they found her dead on the kitchen floor. "I have news," said her minister when she called me that morning. "Mom's gone to the kingdom."

I felt utterly untethered at the death of my mother. Though I haven't done them justice so far, there are many good things to say about her. Mother was a marvelous homemaker, taking pride in the food she served, the clothes she sewed for us, the beauty of her home. We called her Nancy Needles for all the knitwear she made for the family, her hands constantly in motion. I have a favorite picture of Katie and me—she was perhaps three years old—in matching red sweaters Mother knit. I still wear red wool mittens she made for me years ago. She sent each of her five grandchildren to college with an afghan created especially with them in mind, packed into a wooden footlocker my father made for each one. Her first great-grandson, Kurt, wore the tiny blue sweater and booties she had made for his father, Jim, thirty-nine years before.

Her tempers were terrifying to me as a child, but I remember, too, the many days I was sick. She would lay out fresh pajamas and make a clean, smooth bed for me while I took a bath after sweating out a fever. Then she'd bring me baked custard, stepping slowly up the stairs with a tray.

Mother was quick to bake a cake for neighbors fallen into grief. Shy with strangers, she was the hub of the family wheel, the one you called if you wanted to know what was going on with anyone in the wider family. She was always up-to-date on current events, and while my parents were usually of one mind on things, she had a surprising independent streak. I remember the night my father came downstairs from the desk where he had been paying the bills. "What is this check here, Ruth," he inquired, "this one for Planned Parenthood?"

"I wrote that," said Mother. I was stunned. As far as I knew, Mother didn't know how to write a check. For sure, Daddy paid all the bills.

"Ruth, I don't think we should be getting involved in other people's lives like this."

"I wrote that check," stated Mother, fire in her eyes, "and I shall write a check to Planned Parenthood every year of my life."

My father stopped in his tracks, checkbook now hanging limp in his hand. A bewildered look crossed his face. Then he sighed, turned, and retreated up the stairs.

Mother never said a word to me that night, so I have no idea what was behind her determination. We put our heads down and continued reading our books. I will tell you that I have written a check to Planned Parenthood every year of my adult life, my own private Ruth Melson Sparklin memorial.

That exchange was memorable, because I seldom saw my parents in conflict. They were nearly always together, physically and in opinions. One time a therapist asked me what kind of relationship I had with my mother, and I stumbled over the answer. "I don't know that I have a relationship with my mother," I said. "Or my father. I have a relationship with my parents." From the time I left home for college, whenever I phoned home, whoever answered the phone would say, "Wait until I get your…" and then each would get on an extension so as not to miss a thing. That pattern framed our in-person visits as well.

My father's many hospitalizations throughout his long illness were the first occasions when I was alone just with Mother for significant amounts of time. Though scared and often exhausted, she was good company. She and I began to forge an adult friendship of our own. So while on one hand, it wasn't surprising that Mother died so soon after Daddy—the metaphor of a broken heart escaped no one—on the other hand, I grieved for our lost opportunity.

It was a year later that my niece, Barbara, the pastor/counselor in the family, got my sister and me together to talk about our mother and father. We discovered what very different memories we had, what different experiences we had had growing up. What Jean told me that day about her beatings from Mother broke my heart. It also explained a lot.

Working with Susan, I was beginning to understand that the little black girl and the baby of my dreams represented child parts of me I'd lost or abandoned along the way. It wasn't too much of a stretch to frame the Queen of Hearts as the angry mother part of me. I began to appreciate that the terrorists saw their job as keeping me safe. They'd been busy for years keeping me in line, protecting me in the only way they knew—by nurturing my fears, letting me know in no uncertain terms when I was in danger of straying from the Good and Plenty path. That path had been established from birth by my mother's insecurities, and as time went on was stamped more definitively by my own. Stepping off the path led to the terrors of the unknown and to certain punishment; staying on it led to an illusion of safety. It also led to a life of living small, limited by the authority and opinions of others, regardless of whatever personal or professional credibility it might appear I had.

I was determined to live large, and my parents' deaths opened up potential freedom as well as loss. Several years into therapy, I was able to thank the terrorists for "helping" me when I'd needed it, and to tell them I was ready for them to stand aside. I assured them I was now able to take care of my own little girl. They shrugged and slouched off to the edges of my consciousness, smoking cigarettes and leaning on their Uzis. I set off each morning for the forest with my little black girl in hand. I showed her spring trillium, a hemlock tree soaring to the sky with roots exposed, its nurse log long gone. I told her how much I cherished her, assured her that I wanted her with me, that I would keep her safe. As we were walking one morning, I felt the presence of the Queen of Hearts at my side. "You're a good mother," she said. I looked at her, astonished, as she transformed into a wise-older-woman part of me.

Bob, meanwhile, had followed through on his professional plans. When he retired from Weyerhaeuser in 1992, he set up his own firm, the Woodruff Group, and took an office right next to mine in a building at the north end of the island. We worked together with several clients, but billed separately. No one raised an eyebrow at this. We each got to be our own president and secretary. I continued my walks, circling inside the forest each morning, and writing before going to work.

What was I to do about Rachel? I told Bob about my attraction to her and my uncertainty about what to do with it. He told me he trusted me to handle it. She had become a significant partner in my journey toward self-differentiation. Was she meant to be a partner for life? I yearned for a soul mate, a relationship I hadn't experienced, yet believed myself now capable of having. But I hadn't expected a soul mate to show up in a skirt. From the safety of distance I considered the possibility, observing that the terrorists were oiling their guns. By November 1992, the distraction and tension got too great. I told Rachel I didn't think I could be in contact with her any longer. I couldn't hold longing and terror in the same hands, I said. She understood; she said it was hard for her to hold longing and hopelessness in the same hands. We agreed to stop writing, stop phoning. It was painful for both of us. The sorrow I felt at having cut myself off from Rachel's support was nearly unbearable, and of course, no one around me but my therapist knew.

This Pain

Where comes this pain,
deep joy of connection
soul to soul
I turned away from,
keeping the path
of choices made in younger days,
smiling eyes I could not disappoint.

At Susan's suggestion I wore black all through the holidays that December, to honor the heartache I felt inside but could not speak of to anyone. "Wear black," Susan said. "It's a soothing, calming color that looks good on you. Dress it up with the red jacket, with jewelry, scarves, so no one needs to know that you are wearing black because of grief. But you can stay calm in black, and quiet, and that's important. If people know you are grieving, they give you quiet energy. If they don't know, and you can't tell them, you have to create your own quiet energy, so you can have the feelings and get through them." It took all my thespian ability to pull it off, but I did.

On New Year's Day 1993, I dusted myself off and thought, "Whew! Now we can get back on track here."

The Queen of Hearts smiled. The terrorists relaxed. I was going to be Good after all.

Four weeks later, I went to a retreat given by one of my friends. I walked in the door and met Mary Dispenza. Within two weeks, I was in tumult again. It was one thing to have tumult on the East Coast, but here it was standing on my doorstep, willowy, golden, green-eyed, soft-voiced, and radiant.

Chapter 12

THE RETREAT, "Celebrating the Big Five-O," was led by my friend Rita Bresnahan. Rita's goal was to welcome women to their fifties, to honor that yeasty decade. She had asked for my help in the design, help that mainly consisted of my listening to what she had in mind and then saying, "Sounds great!"

"You must come to the workshop," Rita said. "That is how I can pay you."

That's how I happened to walk up the stairs and into a little house in the Ravenna neighborhood of Seattle on Saturday morning, January 29, 1993.

Two other women were already present, hard at work making nametags for themselves. A couple of tables in the entry were strewn with all kinds of supplies for the task, and the two were deep in conversation and laughter as they created showy works of art, bright with curlicues and streamers. Daunted by my lack of artistic talent, I dove in at another table, trimmed brown and green construction paper, pieced them together into what I hoped looked like an apple tree, cut out little red circles for apples and pasted them on.

A dozen of us gathered in a circle to start the day, sitting on the floor of a large comfortable room. We'd each been asked to bring something that symbolized our life at the moment, to create the center of our circle. I had taken a piece of crystal, half-clear and half-cloudy. "I'm in a thirty-two-year-old marriage," I said, placing it on the cloth in the center, "and we are in a time of confusion. Some things are very clear to me, and some things are not, including where our marriage is heading."

One woman—she was one of the nametag artists I met earlier—caught my attention with her honesty, vulnerability, and strength. She began her sharing by commenting that she had recently looked in the mirror and noticed some wrinkles near her eyes. That bothered her. I thought, "But you're beautiful! How could you possibly notice, let alone be bothered by, a tiny wrinkle or two!" She was slender and blonde, with soft green eyes and dimples. All this I took in as I listened. More immediately, she went on, she had come out as a lesbian a year before and lost her job as director of the Pastoral Life Services Department at the Archdiocese of Seattle. She hadn't been able to get any other job since, she said, and that had been hard, particularly since she had spent her entire adult life in service to the Catholic Church. Yet she was at peace. The symbol she brought was a framed quotation from Thoreau: "If I am not I, who will be?"

We had a few words together later than morning in the bathroom line, chuckling that we were both past the need for the session on menopause. She was easy, comfortable. I was—intrigued.

Toward the end of the day, Rita led us in a guided visualization about the women we wanted to be when we were sixty. When that was complete, we paired up with someone to share. Mary (by now I knew her name) and I turned to each other and settled onto the floor in the room next to our meeting room. I was fifty-four, and Mary was fifty-two at the time. I told her my vision of myself at sixty. I had been writing poetry and wanted, by the time I was sixty, to have published a book of poetry. I'd also been writing a haiku each day, after attending a workshop with Angeles Arrien in which she described monks who go out each morning and do not return to the monastery until they have a haiku to bring back. In my meditation, I'd thought to publish a book of my haiku and photography. Then I'd gotten derailed while I nattered to myself about how to do it. I had the woods near my home for the subject, but could I do the photographs? I'd have to get a good camera, I thought, one like my daughter, Katie's. Or maybe I could find a photographer to do that part.

Mary's meditation, she said, had been somewhat muddled by her immediate situation. Not only had she not had an income for months, she had crashed her car that week. It was hard for her to think of tomorrow, let alone to a day she might be sixty. Nonetheless, what she'd like to have done by the age of sixty was to have started a center for arts and spirituality. "Oh," I said, "are you an artist?"

"Yes," she responded.

"What medium do you work in?"

She smiled. "Actually, I'm a photographer."

A few days after Rita's workshop, I mailed my haiku to Mary. She phoned. "I love it. Would you like to come over to see some of my photography?"

February in Seattle always brings one week of brilliant sunshine, a tease amid the misty grayness of winter in the Northwest. This was that week in 1993. I arrived at Mary's house on a sun-splashed weekday morning. Mary met me at the door and invited me to come in. She seemed shy, but warmed as she walked me all around her house—down the hallway to her den, her bedroom, guest room, back into the kitchen and living/dining room with a comfortable sunroom beyond. All was awash in soft color—blues, mauves, pinks, greens—punctuated by art. Photographs, drawings, paintings, and artifacts covered the walls. Mary had spent time in Mexico working at an orphanage and had fallen in love with the people and colors of Mexico. The artifacts were *malecates* she had found on the grounds of the orphanage near the pyramids of Teotihuacán. I saw charcoal sketches of Mother Teresa and Mexican orphans she had done on summer breaks from school. Photographs, too. Mary's brother and niece walked a foggy beach in one, a study in intimacy. The gentle brown eyes of Mexican children reflected the glow of a solitary candle in another. Yet another showed two girls on their tummies, watching ants in the grass, their hair bursting out of barrettes. A triptych of Haleakala volcano at sunrise decorated the laundry room. Photos of green peppers and carrots added splashes of color to her kitchen. Mary laughed from under a straw hat in a photo on the hallway wall, her hand on the wheel of a sailboat, next to the framed quotation that had captured my attention when I first met her: "If I am not I, who will be?"

Alone while Mary prepared brunch, I stood in her living room, listening to the chamber music that filled the house, taking in the beauty and peace of the space. An Indian woman slouched across a bare landscape on horseback on one wall. Warm sun poured in from the other, spotlighting blue-green hydrangeas in a white pitcher and an antique iron horse-drawn fire wagon on the steps to the sunroom. Floral chintz rattan furniture lay beyond the steps. The aroma of Dutch baby pancakes, warming blueberries, and coffee wafted in from the kitchen where Mary was sectioning grapefruit. Looking around, I drew a deep breath, and with the breath one word washed over me: *home*. It was followed by tears.

Followed by panic. You'd better get out of here, I said to myself. This could be trouble.

Pulling Apart

Chapter 13

I STAYED, of course, for the Dutch baby pancakes drenched in warm blueberries, the primrose-decorated grapefruit, coffee, and conversation. I was drawn in by Mary's story. My heart went out to her. So did my admiration. In spite of the depression and economic hardship created by the recent events in her life, she had embraced her newly claimed sexual orientation with joy. She had made a whole new set of friends, she was on the board of Hands Off Washington, a grass roots organization fighting an initiative on our state ballot to restrict the rights of gay, lesbian, bisexual, and transgender (GLBT) persons. I was stunned by the complexity of her life and the honor shining through it. And there were those soft green eyes, the warm smile.

I left Mary's that day with all caution lights flashing inside. The terrorists in me, those Uzi-toting guys in battle fatigues whose job it was to keep me in line and safe, came to attention and began to mark time with their boots. Everything in me screamed, "Stay away from this!" No, not everything. An unspoken knowing, that sense of home I felt in my guts, called me back.

In another couple of weeks, I invited Mary to come for a walk in my woods, pursuing the idea of doing the book of haiku and photography together. We walked around Pioneer Park near my home on the south end of Mercer Island, while I showed her the path of my haiku, the tall Doug firs and hemlocks, the nurse logs, thicket bushes just beginning to bud, the spot where the trillium would appear, all scenes she could photograph for the book. She took a bunch of pictures, printed them out later in black and white. That was as far as we got with the project.

While we walked, we talked. She was one of the most forthcoming persons I had ever met. Nothing was off-limits to share, and she had a fascinating story. She was raised in East Los Angeles. She had been sexually abused by a priest as a young girl and had, only two years before, become conscious of her abuse. With assistance from a Catholic therapy group in Seattle, she then had arranged for the priest to come to Seattle for a three-day confrontation process. She still bore the emotional pain of her abuse. As a child, she had felt the kindness of the nuns who were her teachers, and she loved them, as she did her overworked, alcoholic mother. She became a Roman Catholic nun right out of high school. She stayed with the Religious of the Sacred Heart of Mary for fifteen years, becoming a teacher and a principal, obtaining a BA and then a master's degree. After leaving her religious community, she had a successful career as a parochial school principal before being selected by Archbishop Hunthausen to be head of Seattle's Pastoral Life Services Department—from which she'd been fired a year before I met her for coming out as a lesbian in the *Seattle Times*. There was a vulnerability about Mary that I wanted to protect. There was an inner strength about her that I deeply admired.

Shortly after I met Mary, I was in San Francisco for work. Unable to get her story out of my mind, I dashed off a poem. Writing poetry was often the way I was able to understand or digest an experience that moved me, and this was one of those experiences. When I returned to Seattle and read the poem to Mary, she was very quiet. I had heard her.

Hello, Church

(dedicated, with great respect, to someone who is saying good-bye)

When I was a young girl you raped me
and I kept quiet.
I took on the shame myself, protected you,
denied my knowing that you were wrong, terribly wrong,
silenced my own child's truth,
embodied your guilt, made it mine—
and lost my voice.

So eager was I, desperate even, for the love you promised,
the comfort and acceptance shining in your eyes,
the chance you offered to help me make sense
of my senseless world,
I muzzled my hysteria, followed the rules,
hid myself, hushed myself, became *not me*,
so that *not me* might be loved by you.

I grew up, chose to stay with you.
I did a lot of good in your name,
spoke with your voice of love and redemption
but silenced my own because it spoke to me of longings
that were "the bane of community,"
and I needed community to salve my wounded soul.

You who sheltered me, gave me position,
framed my life work in your body,
also imprisoned me in your terrible darkness,
and the secret knowledge of my own.

Finally, shaman-like, I retrieved my soul,
reclaimed the self I'd buried in my chambered chaos,
called me—tremulous, triumphant--
into the light.

"The truth shall set you free," I heard
and, daring to trust,
I cleared my throat, spoke my truth…
and you raped me again.

This time I'll not be silent.
No longer a child,
having found my woman voice
I will speak out.

You're on your own
with your shame and guilt
this time.

Chapter 14

MARY AND I continued to meet now and then. She asked me one day to go for a hike at Denny Creek, one of her favorite places. As I drove and we talked, she casually placed her hand on my thigh. I felt my heart jump as electricity flooded my body. I said nothing; I couldn't speak.

Many days we'd have coffee and talk, and talk, and talk. Her place or mine. The level of intimacy between us took my breath away. I could tell her anything. One day Bob came home while Mary and I were sitting at the kitchen table over coffee. I introduced them. Later Bob said to me, "Is this another Rachel?"

"Oh no," I said, and I meant it. Bob was probably reassured, but I knew this new friendship was different in a way I couldn't express even to myself. Beneath being interested in her as a friend and wanting to know her better was a now familiar sense of urgency. A resonance with something buried in me that was rising and would be seen. When I got close to that resonance, I was terrified. My soul was on fire and my body followed, though I tried to keep it quiet.

I told Mary that I was committed to my marriage. She said she didn't intend to come between the two of us. I told her I was working on myself in therapy, and Bob was working on himself. We were works in progress, I said, and I was committed to the process. Still... I couldn't help but notice how easy the process was between the two of us.

Several months after we first met, Mary came over to my house. She wanted to discuss why it probably wasn't a good idea for us to continue seeing each other. I, after all, was married. It was clear that we were attracted to each other, but my being married was a complication that needed to be honored. Perhaps it was a mistake to consider we could even be friends. The thing to do, she said, was for her to bow out of the picture until things got clearer for Bob and me. We were sitting in our family room, Mary on the red plaid sofa facing the fireplace, I on a big chair, my feet on a hassock, facing Mary. Behind Mary I regarded the library table laden with family pictures: Bob and me, Jim and Katie in all their growing-up years—the soccer teams, the play costumes, the Christmas card photos. Baron Grinnit, our miniature schnauzer, snored on the red Irish wool rug in front of the fireplace. The Woodruff family dream in all its fullness. What Mary was saying made all the sense in the world. What she proposed was the right thing to do.

Then I leaned over, took Mary's hand, and pulled her across the space between the sofa and the hassock. I held her in my arms and put one hand on her head. "I just wanted to know," I whispered, "what your hair would feel like." We barely breathed, held absolutely still in our embrace, knowing that any move, in any direction, would tip us into a shining possibility, a terrifying possibility. We wrestled with how to act with integrity. We backed away from each other. Yet she was already vibrating in every corner of my being.

Bob and I were also wrestling with how to act with integrity. In therapy, individually and as a couple, we were making strides in getting clear about our own issues, continuing the work of self-differentiation begun at the WeirLab, addressing how to be professional colleagues and at the same time maintain enough space so we both could do our own work, and that had to be our priority. I was writing, writing, dialoguing with those parts of me I've already named. I don't know what Bob's work involved, but I knew he was deep into it.

Bob and I never stopped talking while teetering on the horns of our dilemma. I believe Bob and I did the best we could at honoring our relationship and our history while confronting the realities before us. We were honest with each other as much as we could be. Yet it was becoming clear that what we each needed and wanted might not be possible for the other to give without losing the selves we were working so hard to gain. And that made us very sad.

The Explorer and the Writer

An explorer and a writer sat at the kitchen table
speaking their dreams.

I want the world, said the explorer,
his eyes sparkling with enthusiasm,
I want to see everything,
taste everything,
have everything.
This is my time, an exciting time,
my bags are packed, I'm ready,
come with me.

The writer felt exhausted.

I want solitude, said the writer,
her eyes fired with determination,
I want to know everything,
feel everything,
understand everything.
I'm on a journey to my soul, an interior time,
I need solace and peace while I work
to come home.

The explorer felt confused.

An explorer and a writer sat at the kitchen table
speaking their dreams;
the north and the south winds
blew at the door.

Chapter 15

IT WAS INCONCEIVABLE to me that Bob and Mary Ann Woodruff wouldn't stay married. We were, after all, that kind of couple. We would work things out. We would celebrate our fiftieth wedding anniversary, with any luck, with both of our children, their spouses, and our grandchildren, perhaps with a week together at a big house we would rent in Hawaii. We only had seventeen years to go. No one in our family got divorced, and we certainly couldn't. It was clear, though, that the fabric of our marriage was becoming frayed. And at the same time, it was also clear to me that I couldn't, or wouldn't, let go of Mary.

That summer, July 1993, I went to Flight of the Mind, a women's writer's retreat on the Mackenzie River in central Oregon. I took a poetry workshop from Judith Barrington, who challenged us with a call to integrity. "The poet's job," she said, "is to write the truth. And then write the truth below the truth."

Struggling to acknowledge the truth, let alone to write about it, I found a form that could contain the swirling emotions inside. The form was *pantoum*, a four-line stanza poem where the second and fourth lines of one stanza become the first and third lines of the next until the last stanza, where the first and third lines of the first stanza are repeated, in reverse order. The circularity of the form served to help me peel the onion of the truth below the truth.

Pantoum for a Marriage

I'm not ready to let go of this marriage.
We were friends before we were lovers,
we support each other, are good to each other
thirty-three years, five homes, two grown children,
    thousands of memories.

We were friends before we were lovers;
laughter, talking and faith sustain us
thirty-three years, five homes, two grown children,
    thousands of memories:
the joyous, painful stuff of life.

Laughter, talking and faith sustain us;
through deaths of first born son, parents, and illusions
the joyous, painful stuff of life,
we create safe harbor.

Through deaths of first born son, parents, and illusions
we hang in, solid, through thick and thin
we create safe harbor
people feel whole around us, they say.

We hang in, solid, through thick and thin
we love what we are when together in public.
People feel whole around us, they say,
but loneliness rises like steam when the doors close.

We love what we are when together in public.
In private we grow cautious, polite with each other,
and loneliness rises like steam when the doors close;
we give our best to others.

In private we grow cautious, polite with each other,
the anger erupts violently, we are frightened,
we give our best to others
and lie awake at 3:00 in the morning.

The anger erupts violently, we are frightened,
we wonder if we will make it for the second half
and lie awake at 3:00 in the morning
praying for wisdom.

We wonder if we will make it for the second half;
we support each other, are good to each other.
Praying for wisdom
I'm not ready to let go of this marriage.

Chapter 16

CONVENTIONAL WISDOM says that it makes sense to end one relationship before starting another. Conventional wisdom says that you commit to your first relationship, stay with it either until it is better, or until it is clear that better is no longer possible. Then you come to a tidy ending and enter a fallow period. Alone, you have a chance to grieve, regroup, get your feet under you, and become clear about your priorities. Then, and only then, goes conventional wisdom, are you ready to entertain the notion of a new relationship.

Well, there's conventional wisdom—and then there's life. In our case, the messy truth was that everything burst open at the same time: challenges with our marriage, Bob's leaving corporate life and striking out on his own as a consultant, our being in therapy trying to sort out who we were and how we'd be in the decade of our fifties, my meeting Mary.

I'd like to say that I gave my absolute all to working things out with Bob, that he gave his absolute all to working things out with me. But the truth is that we both were distracted, though I more than Bob, and sooner. While Mary vowed she didn't intend to come between us, the attraction was stronger than common sense, and I couldn't deny it. Never had I known such joy, such openness. Guiltily I moved toward her, all the while trying to be honest with myself and with Bob, working on our issues in couple's therapy. It was intoxicating... and terrifying.

In touching Mary's hair, I had opened Pandora's box. Each time she smiled at me, her eyes fell into my soul. My hands itched to touch her when she was away, my body yearned to bury itself in hers when she was near. I was awash in feelings. The terrorists yammered in my head, pointing out that I was headed toward violating sacred vows, and there would be hell to pay if I did. I was not the type to do so lightly, and I didn't. Yet something else was going on, too. An inescapable imperative was working me like a still, small voice in the night. As time went on, and in the course of many conversations, Mary offered her wisdom. It was the old-soul quality of her I so respected. If I were questioning my sexuality, she said, it would be hard to answer such questions with thinking and talking alone. She commented, "There are some things that you cannot know until you experience them."

What would it be like to make love with a woman? To know that level of intimacy with a woman? To act on all the longing that quickened the beat of my heart and made it sing when I was near her? Those questions simmered in my head when I was busy with other parts of my life. They boiled when I was with Mary. It was as if I would die if I didn't try to answer them. One day, sitting in her backyard and scarcely able to breathe for the tension, I blurted, "Mary, will you take me to bed?" She did.

I couldn't find words to express what it was like.

"Give me some metaphors," said Susan.

You Asked for Metaphors

I.
I hurl myself into the oncoming wave
up, up, exhilarated,
I'm lifted, carried on the swell
shoreward, thrown
on the sand, a tangle
of bubbles and laughter,
struggle to regain my footing,
am brought down
again and again
in the grinding surf,
breathless,
joyful,
spent.

II.
It's been a long walk, a long hot journey
on this dry, bone-baked desert sand.
Parched, sweat soaked,
hair matted under the blankets that protect me
from the sun,
I swear it is a mirage:
green shade trees,
sounds of running water,
and as I approach, a cool breeze
freshens my face.

Someone comes to meet me with a glass and pitcher.
I drink and drink deeply,
slaking a thirst greater than I knew I had.
A hand leads me to a cool grotto
where a clear pool awaits,
fed by crystal waterfalls;

I unwrap my musky coverings,
peel off layers of dust and dryness,
marvel at the feel of fragrant, soft air
on my skin,
then, as I take courage,
slip my body into the pool
and float, tension easing,
in the stillness.

III.

A universe of stars overhead,
timeless acceptance,
witnesses
this mystery.

Chapter 17

Returning to my home was unsettling. I had been shaken to the core, I was wordless, and here I was back in the kitchen on Eighty-Third Place, here I was making dinner and sharing it with Bob, here I was back in bed with the man who had been my beloved husband for years and years. The man I so hoped could become the soul mate for whom I yearned.

Bedtime Story

> In the early dawn I turn to you,
> press my body the length of yours,
> curl my arm around your waist,
> feel the familiar ins and outs
> of this body I know so well.
>
> Lying here, I draw strength and comfort
> from your solidness.
> I ground myself in your dependability,
> your steadfastness,
> your optimism, and encouragement.

> How is it, in the midst of all this richness,
> I can lie here
> feeling such sadness,
> such longing?

Bob and I continued in couple's therapy, discussing our new realities and the support we each needed while we processed all these challenges. I tried to be as honest as I could be about my feelings for Mary, but it was difficult, because they so threatened our security. I was alternately dazzled and drenched in dread.

Jim and his girlfriend, Jonae, were with us through Christmas 1993, visiting from Munich where Jim's work with Intel had taken him. Katie was with us, too, on holiday break from graduate school in public health at Berkeley. We had a fine time, although there was this giant elephant in the living room, lounging beside the Christmas tree.

"You know, I'll be leaving soon," said Jim, toward the end of his stay. "This has been great, but there's more that you two aren't talking about. I hate the thought of going back to Germany with things unsaid. Can't you tell us what's really going on?"

Bob and I said yes and set a time for us to talk. Came the time, we sat down in the living room—Jim, Katie, Bob, and I. Jonae had excused herself and gone upstairs to her room, giving us Woodruffs space.

Bob explained that we had been having trouble in our marriage, and that we were in therapy together as well as in individual therapy. "I'd like to reassure you that we'll get through this and come out OK on the other side," he said to Jim and Katie, "but I'm not sure that I can. I can tell you that we're hard at work on it."

Both Katie and Jim were quick to offer their support. Don't do or not do anything because of us, Katie said. We're big kids, we're grown ups. We'll be OK, whatever you need to do, as long as no one gets kicked out of the family.

It was quiet in the living room. I was in the wing chair facing the fireplace. Katie and Bob sat at either ends of the sofa to my left, in front of the window. Jim was in the rocking chair opposite me.

"There's one more thing," I croaked, clearing my throat. "I've met this woman. You both know I've always had good woman friends, but this is different, far different from, say, my friendship with Carol." I took a breath. "I don't know where it's going, and I'm afraid to even say a word about it because I'm scared everyone is going to run out of the room."

Now it was *really* quiet.

Jim pulled his six-foot-three frame up from where he was sitting and walked across the room to me. He dropped to the floor, put his arms around my legs, and laid his head on my knee. "No one's going anywhere, Mom," he said.

Chapter 18

IT WOULD BE LOVELY to claim that with our children's support things went smoothly for us after that. But that would be untrue. It was a messy, ragged time.

Bob pleaded with me, "Play me or trade me." He had found someone in whom he was interested, and if I didn't want him, he was ready to move on, he said.

I was too terrified to own my feelings for Mary, too frozen with fear—and too married!—to be ready to do any trading. I knew I wanted a soul mate. Mary could be that. But I wanted Bob to be my soul mate; it was hard to let go of that dream. In therapy, he told me he wasn't interested in being my soul mate. "I'll go as deep as I can," he pledged. "But I just don't go very deep."

"Look, Mary Ann," he said one day. "If this is the way you want to go with your life, I'll support you, and you'll never hear a bad word from me about it."

I stared at him in disbelief. How could I say this was the way I wanted to go with my life? Who would want this—the shunning, the shame, the possible loss of friends, alienation from the community?

Where does homophobia come from? I didn't learn it from my parents. I've already mentioned Leonard, the debonair gay man who joined the Trosch family for many Christmases when I was young. If my parents were bothered by Leonard, I never heard it. And by the time I was an adult, when the topic of the ordination of gay Presbyterians as ministers, elders, or deacons came up in conversations with my parents, they were always in favor. As was I. I have discovered, however, that it is one thing to be a liberal-minded person who has compassion for others and quite another thing to fancy oneself being one of those "others."

When I first began to tell friends about Mary and my angst over where my feelings might take me, to a person each one responded with tenderness, some version of, "I've always loved you. Why would this change my love for you?" Each of these conversations was a blessing to me. But my inner dialogue was brutal. It slammed me awake nights, sweating. It sent me to the living room, where I huddled in the wing chair staring into the fireplace, seeing nothing.

All my life I'd been on the privileged side of almost any equation I could name: American, white, Christian, raised in plenty, well educated, well married, with children who were untroubled and trustworthy. Even being a woman had scarcely had a serious downside for me. But being a lesbian? Not only did that conjure up some unattractive images I didn't want to relate to, it also brought me face to face with my own heterosexism. In my heart of hearts, beating right along with my growing love, my desire for Mary, lurked a presumption that heterosexuals are superior to homosexuals, that GLBT persons are second-class citizens. I moved easily in the world as a married woman, unconscious until now of heterosexual privilege. Marriage afforded me a certain status, a comfortable belonging that the world assumed was good. And our marriage was very good—until it wasn't. I believed I didn't want to lose Bob, and I was hardly able to tell myself how much was about losing him, the person, and how much was about losing my long-accustomed security. I didn't want to lose the privilege of marriage, either.

And then there was the church. I had been an elder in the Presbyterian Church for some fifteen years. I had served on several presbytery committees, had chaired a couple, had consulted with conflicted churches or ones wanting to know how to begin a long-range planning process. I was consulting on strategic planning with the Presbyterian Church General Assembly Council in Louisville, the highest body in the church, for heaven's sake, while struggling with the dilemma of Mary (all the while thinking, Oh, if you only knew...). As a representative of my church at presbytery, I had voted in favor of liberalizing the standards for ordination of pastors, elders, and deacons and had been dismayed each time the progressive side was defeated. In my own presbytery, I knew there were people I respected and who respected me who, if they knew of my love for a woman, would judge me to be beyond the pale. I told someone it felt as though my whole life were a stack of poker chips, one a lot of people would consider a pretty fine stack. But if this one extra chip were added to the stack—that I loved Mary and was considering being her partner—the whole stack would crumble into a useless pile. I could no longer serve the church as an elder if I were in a relationship with a woman. The church was huge in my life. How could I do anything to break that defining connection? To say yes to being with Mary would be to lose the church, and that alone was enough to paralyze me.

The church's way of settling conflicts was no help. When Presbyterians consider an issue, our *Book of Order* directs that to do it "decently and in order," we must place a motion on the floor and ask those who wish to comment to step up to either of two opposing microphones and speak for or against the motion. At the end of the debate we vote, ensuring that the winners triumph, the losers sulk in corners and plan to fight another day. In this "orderly" dualism, everything becomes either right or wrong, true or false, good or evil, win or lose. This habit of either/or thinking caught me up short as I wrestled with loving Mary. As far as I knew, I had loved Bob with all my heart until things began to change. Was I straight or gay? Had I been a lesbian all along who lived a lie with my husband? Was I going against my own nature in being so attracted to Mary? What was true, what was false? I tortured myself with these questions.

Later, when I stilled my monkey mind and listened for the voice of God, that voice released me to be myself, unique and beloved in the same way each of God's creatures is. Now I hear Bob's offer with all the grace with which he made it. Then, I gave my fear the upper hand. There was too much at stake. The cringing little kid in me was coming undone. I resolved to get myself back in line. The terrorists breathed more easily.

Fear Fall

> A small truth perches on my lips
> like an unbalanced fledgling
> teetering in terror at the edge of the nest,
> its fantasy feeding fear of either flight or fall.
>
> Around and around it totters,
> wishing it could return to the egg,
> reconstruct the protective shell now shattered,
> regain the safe darkness of undiscovery.

Naked, damp, it shivers in the cold breeze,
ruffles its feathers for courage,
lifts off as though to jump and have it out—
then pulls back, panting, panicked.

Chapter 19

MARY OFFERED ME grace as well. "I love you. I desire you," she said. "Just take it in, just take it in. I love your mind, your heart, your soul. I love your sensitivity, your warmth, your body. Don't get scared by this. I want to say that if, and it's a big if, we were ever to consider partnership, I know it would have to come after you have decided on your own path. And if you need space to find that path, whatever it is, I am ready to give it to you." She gave me a beautiful gold heron pendant, to remind me that she would wait for me, unless and until a time came when she felt it was no longer healthy for her to do so.

Mary was hard at work getting her employment situation back on track. Having been booted out of the Chancery department, she first looked to return to Catholic schools, where she had been named a national distinguished principal. She was told, however, that she was, in effect, blackballed by the church for the way she had come out, and that no Catholic institution would or could hire her. She tried anything for work after that—diversity training, multilevel marketing, educational consulting—continuing to search for the right place to use her gifts. She was also thoroughly committed to her activism on behalf of GLBT persons. It was clear there could be no smallness in a permanent relationship with her, no story of two "women friends" who just happened to live together.

The WeirLab had taught me that the greatest resistance to self-differentiation is fear. If you encounter parts of yourself that are new or heretofore unrecognized, the fear of rejection can make acceptance impossible. Fear of knowing, or of having to be responsible for the new knowledge, can keep you from acknowledging it. Finally, fear of failure can make you resist executing your new self with authority, even if you've accepted and acknowledged it to yourself—"I've never done it this way so I'll probably screw it up." I had every fear named by the WeirLab and then some. I could see my life moving on without love, without relationship, because of my fear. The terrorists had me in their grips again. Whatever Samurai warrior I thought I had inside to do battle for me had taken a long hike.

In the midst of all this anguish, I fell out of bed one morning onto my knees, pressed my face into the gold-and-white toile print of our bedspread, and wailed, "I can't do this anymore! I cannot do this alone."

"Whoever said you had to?" said a voice, clear as a bell in my head. I had the sense of a Presence walking across a meadow toward me, opening a gate, and coming closer, smiling. I surrendered to that Presence and begged for help, an action I would need to repeat over and over, but one that never failed me when I called on it.

I prayed my heart out asking for wisdom. Bob ran out of patience before I ran out of denial. In August 1994, he moved out of our home. I stumbled around in shock and kept Mary at a distance.

I Need to Be by Myself

Did I tell you how a closet looks half empty?
How the refrigerator looks without the Mariners' schedule?
The family room wall without the family faces?
Did I tell you how my heart feels half empty,
my stomach full of bile and fear,
my thoughts a jumble?
 Did I tell you I need to be by myself for a while?

I don't know, right now, who I am.
Have I screwed up my life irreversibly?
Have I made a true choice and am just now having trouble
    living with it?
Have I let fantasy run away with reality?
Have I lost my soul, battling with my head, my critics, and my
    fears?
Where am I, who am I, how will I be?
 Did I tell you I need to be by myself for a while?

You are warm, soft, a great comfort.
You hold me tenderly, listen without judgment, smile me into
    response.
I swell, I move into you again and again
and I don't know if I am moving toward you
or away from this panic, shielding myself with you,
not facing what I need to face in me.
 Did I tell you I need to be by myself for a while?

I need to be just here, in these dark woods,
face these doubts, walk these fears, answer the questions.
I need to know that I can stand here
or that I can't.
It is time and I have created the space
for this next piece of the journey.
  Did I tell you I need to be by myself for a while?

In the fall of that year, my acupuncturist invited me to study the philosophy behind the traditional Chinese acupuncture she applied to me. "After all, Mary Ann," Kim pointed out, "isn't your work in organizations about finding the places where energy is stuck and then determining the right intervention to get it flowing again?" Intrigued, I joined the year-long SOPHIA (School of Philosophy and Healing in Action) program of the Traditional Acupuncture Institute.

Right away, I learned about the five seasons at the core of traditional Chinese acupuncture. Spring is the season of new beginnings, new vision, green shoots just emerging. Summer, the season of flowering, is also the season of fire, of partnerships for the sake of a sovereign mission. Late summer is the season of harvest and acknowledgement of the fruits of what began in the spring. Autumn is the season of letting go, the season of grief, of pruning the garden for the sake of its life. Winter is the season of fallowness when one nearly drowns in the fear of the unknown; it is the time to breathe with one's unanswered questions, listening for answers from within. Each season is identified with a distinct element (wood, fire, earth, metal, water) and emotion. Each season governs different systems in or parts of the body. Separating from Bob brought autumn to my heart. Grieving, I struggled with letting go, not sure of which part of me to lop off for the sake of my life.

SOPHIA also taught me about the power of declaration. I declared to myself that Bob and I were a partnership for life, no matter what. Our children, values, and work in common would keep us so. I knew that whether that partnership would be in the form of marriage or not was too small a conversation. I declared that Mary and I were a partnership for life as well, no matter what. The depth and joy of our connection made us so, regardless of the form that partnership would take.

The big conversation for me, though, was not about partnership with either Bob or Mary. I could frame my dilemma as that, but the truth beneath the truth was that the partnership I needed to find and declare was with myself. Could I do that? And would I?

Chapter 20

LATE ONE AFTERNOON in March 1995, Bob and I settled into our counselor's room, I on the sofa, Bob in a chair at a ninety-degree angle to me. Our counselor (I'll call her Margo) smiled at each of us from her own chair across from us. We had come to do a ritual for letting go of our marriage. Bob's patience had run its course; he needed to move on. I couldn't give him a genuine reason not to.

Margo had asked us each to think of three things we needed to ask forgiveness for from each other, and three things that we would take away as blessings from our time together.

We began.

- I asked Bob to forgive me for refusing him on Woodruff Associates, for the hurt that caused him.

- He asked me to forgive him for not knowing how to be emotionally with me and then leaving me shortly after he "discovered what it was all about."

- I asked Bob to forgive me for the sense of abandonment he experienced when I began to write and take space for solitude.

- He asked me to forgive him for not seeing and appreciating that my writing is me and is a window to my "true, beautiful heart."

- I asked Bob to forgive me for infidelity.
- He asked me to forgive him for not listening to me and always justifying his actions.

It would be impossible to put into words the relief that these requests brought. To hear Bob acknowledge some of the deepest pain I experienced in our relationship, to hear him honor my writing and my soul's longing for communion with him was a blessed moment. And I think the same was true for him. We cried and cried. Then we moved on to blessings.

Bob's words to me: I've been blessed by:

- Your wonderful creative gifts, personally created. The EAST WEST, HOME'S BEST and THE WOODRUFF MACHINERY MANUFACTURING COMPANY were both beautiful and not always fully appreciated.
- Your wanting to be always open, until I shut you down. You wanted more love than I was able to give.
- Your willingness to try some new things such as sailing—have at it! You aren't afraid—go for it.

My words to him: I've been blessed by:

- Your optimism. You believed in me when I didn't believe in myself. I leaned on your optimism and was fed by it. Your optimism also helped my mother, especially when Daddy was sick. You were a wonderful son-in-law, and they loved you very much.

- Your trust. You trusted me, and I tried to live up to your trust. Your trust in other people is a blessing you give to the world. Your trust in Jim and Katie has helped make them the special people they are. You've been an exceptional father and husband because of your trust in all of us.

- Your faith. It has been wonderful that we shared so much the same faith in God, that we've been together in the church community. When times were tough, our mutual faith sustained us—we had the same framework of belief, and that's been a blessing.

With Margo's guidance, we had done a thorough job of acknowledging the late-summer fruits of our marriage. Gracefully and with compassion she led us in separating that day.

Rings
Diamonds sapphires and white gold around my finger binding a ring in my flesh, rings say I have been chosen, owned in a way, safe in a way I'm not now, rings are marks on table tops we don't want to have, the belts around Saturn, dirt around a shirt collar, things to toss at pointy objects that just stand there and don't do a thing to catch the rings, what you grab for as your carousel horse goes around, up and down, what a bell does to remind you that it's time, time for mass, time to greet the morning, time to answer the door and greet

a visitor, I ring you up to say hello and make a date or tell you I'm thinking of you, Ring Around the Rosy is a game we played as kids and we all fell down laughing, rings...symbols of eternity, the eternal circle with no beginning and no end, the symbol of marriage but of course it has a beginning and it seems this one has an end and that's the bitter joke of this, that no one is laughing because there is something unnatural about taking off your rings when you are still alive and very good friends and as far as I can tell, at some level, in love.

Fast forward to December 5, 1995, the day we were to go to court to finalize our divorce. Bob and I met at the Four Seasons Hotel in Seattle, one of the most elegant places in the city, for breakfast. We walked into the Georgian Room where the hostess said brightly to Bob, "I've given you a special table, because you said this was a special occasion."

"Yes," boomed Bob, "we're getting a divorce today!" I flinched, willing to go along with making something significant of the occasion but feeling anything but celebratory. I felt disoriented.

Without conferring ahead of time, we each had brought a gift for the other. I gave Bob a jade apple and talked about the soft inside that I had valued in him. He gave me a Swarovski dove of peace and told me he wished to make peace, and he wished me peace for the future.

We finished breakfast, then walked down the street to collect the lawyer who had worked up the papers for us. The three of us proceeded to the courthouse, Bob chatting easily with the lawyer. I was numb. Sitting in the hallway before we went into the courtroom, I said, "Bob, do we really have to do this?" He nodded. And so we went in when it was our turn, papers were read, a decree issued by the judge, and our thirty-five-year marriage was over.

Afterward Bob moved right along with his new love (I'll call her Pamela) with never, as far as I could see, a backward glance. And I now was free to explore partnership with Mary. There was no doubt that I loved her. Mary had a playful, funny side to her as well as an old-soul wisdom; I was attracted to both. With her I felt a joy, a trust, an intimacy that was natural and marvelous. Yet while Mary was dedicated to living out and proud, I was still nearly strangled with homophobia. And a great sense of the loss of our marriage.

Our house on Mercer Island had been up for sale for some time and finally sold in early 1996. Bob and Pamela had gone off to Egypt, and he wanted nothing to do with clearing out the house or taking care of the belongings in it. That made me furious. Katie and Mary helped me hold a garage sale, and we weeded out things right and left. I was in an altered state, fueled by anger. I remember Katie saying, "You can't give your wedding dress away in a garage sale!" I think she took it. But I was a little nuts at the time, and I put nearly everything else into the sale. Handmade quilts, family heirlooms, boxes and boxes of slides—we had a closet of them from when Bob was taking photos, and some from his father too, but if he didn't want any of them, I didn't intend to store them in whatever little space I would have until he might.

Shortly after this, Mary and I had the gift of a friend's cabin at Hood Canal. I remember dissolving into tears and spending hours sobbing on one of the beds for most of a day, wave after wave of grief rising and pouring out. Mary lit a candle and sat in the living room, bearing witness and staying out of my way. It is one of her gifts to me that she never asked for an explanation. She just gave me space and was there to be with me when I emerged.

Low Tide

I, ocean,
distance myself again and again
pile up in the middle of nowhere
a raging boil of emotion
spit foam and fury from the tips of my swells
—I'm deep, so proudly deep—
beware the deadly behemoths
rampaging beneath my surface.

You, beach,
anchored to the shore
lie open and without guile
your secrets exposed
to eyes and feet that probe your sandbars,
you shelter life in the shallows
nourish horse clams, great blue heron, Bonaparte gulls,
and patiently wait, gathering warmth,

for my inevitable
return.

Going In

Chapter 21

IN MARCH 1996, I moved to a rental house off East Mercer Way. To get to the house, you drove up a narrow, winding lane to a landing space in the woods. There, nestled among big leaf maple trees was a small, one-story home with a carport. The living-dining room's south wall was filled with windows rising to a lofted ceiling, with all of nature outdoors shining in. A wood-burning fireplace and hearth on the north wall faced the windows. My seven "chosen sisters," women I'd known for more than twenty years, helped me on moving day and didn't leave until they had the living room and bedroom set up. They arranged our old family room furniture—the plaid sofa, the Mount Holyoke rocker I won in a reunion raffle, the large cream chairs and hassock, and the Irish wool rug—around and under the large glass-topped coffee table from our living room in a grouping before the fireplace. On the walls we hung Sparklin/Melson family heirlooms: the portrait of my mother as a young girl, the wedding certificate of her mother's parents, the Sparklin family crest my father's sister, Edith, dreamed up. It's not authentic, but it gives me a chuckle.

It was the first time in my life that I lived on my own. I was fifty-seven years old. It was the first time I could have a home just the way I wanted it, experience the freedom to do my life the way I wanted. It was wonderful space—light, with a yard in which I could dance naked if I wanted without being seen or disturbed, a bird feeder outside my study, room for the piano, a guest room. It was a perfect place to come back to, a place to find myself.

She Wraps the House Around Her

She wraps the house around her.
Arriving at the top of the lane,
she stills her engine,
unlocks the door, and
sinks into sunlight,
flowers, fireplace,
music.

She wraps the house around her,
quietly sits in the crook of its arm,
smells pungent grasses, watches trees burst,
waits for the eagle she once saw
circling overhead to return,
listens to buzz of planes, insects,
beat of her own heart.

She wraps the house around her.
Solitude like she has never known
is her companion now.
At night she dims the lamps,
settles into the couch, her eyes
on lights across the lake;
she is rising from a deep well.

> She wraps the house around her,
> cooks a gourmet feast
> for friends who midwifed her,
> celebrating, with champagne
> and laughter,
> the miracle
> of resurrection.

Mary of course figured prominently in that house, too. We were freer to think about a future now, to try that on, to loll around outside in my tree-lined yard and dream together. I loved her more and more but still needed time, still held back from total commitment.

You Love Me Bigger

You love me bigger than I expect to be loved.
Again and again you spread your palms,
blow me loose with your sweet breath,
smile me floating into the freedom
of myself.

You love me bigger than I deserve.
You hear my struggle and respond with
understanding, tenderly repackage my words
so I hear myself making more sense
than I knew I could.

You love me bigger than I know how to say.
Before your wisdom I am silent—
a child, a student.
I stand in awe of your selfless teaching,
your generous love.

You love me bigger
than I know how to be.

Chapter 22

JIM AND JONAE came to Seattle from Munich, where they were still living, for Christmas 1996. They were engaged to be married on September 20, 1997, and the family gathered to celebrate their engagement and plan for the wedding. The family included Jonae's mother, Tanene, her sister, Janelle, Katie, Bob, Pamela, Mary, and me.

It snowed that Christmas—a lot. We had an engagement party for Jim and Jonae at my house. Rosie Seeks, our caterer from down the way, recruited her kids to help her bring the food up to the house by sled. Those who could slog through the snow arrived in ski pants and sweaters. It was a happy occasion.

On Christmas day, we all met at Bob and Pamela's house so Jim and Jonae could share their plans for their wedding weekend. Given the number of family and their friends who would be coming for the wedding from all over the world, Jim and Jonae had several things in mind: the rehearsal and dinner for the wedding party on Thursday night, an Oktoberfest-type celebration for all out-of-town guests and family on Friday night. They were to be married on Saturday, at Bob's church, Plymouth Congregational, with a reception at the Women's University Club, just a short post-wedding walk up Sixth Avenue in Seattle.

Things got awkward when the question came up about Pamela and Mary's roles. Pamela had moved in with Bob, but they were not entirely solid about their direction. Mary and I were still not clear about our direction either. It would be clear to everyone that Pamela and Bob were romantic partners. But how to introduce Mary? Jim and Jonae saved the day by asking Mary to take pictures of the entire weekend and especially to follow the photographer around on their wedding day and take black-and-white pictures. She'd be introduced to Jonae's and Bob's family as my friend and traveling companion.

My family and my close friends knew about Mary, and they had all been supportive. Bob's family, however, didn't have a clue. His mother and sister held the story that Bob left me for a younger woman, and they were angry. From Eddie Woodruff's perspective, our problem was that Bob was too "cock of the walk," and I was too much of a feminist. Why couldn't we just admit it and get on with our lives together? Bob's sister and her husband had become evangelical Christians in recent years, and I didn't want to imagine what they would do if they knew I was flirting with being a lesbian. I knew I loved Mary, but I wasn't sure enough yet about my commitment to her to risk the uproar that was sure to ensue if they were to find out. I didn't want to spoil Jim and Jonae's special time by our being a distraction. I was a wreck.

Bob was a wreck as well. He had taken Pamela to Savannah to meet his family before we were divorced, and the meeting hadn't gone as he had hoped. His mother, sister, and brother-in-law were cold, furious at both Bob and me because we weren't able to work out our differences, and upset that he'd jumped into a new relationship before things were settled between us. Bob had kept his tongue and taken the blame. But now, with the wedding approaching, he wanted me to let them know my part in our breakup. "If you don't tell them," he sputtered to me one day, "I will. I don't want them to come to Jim and Jonae's wedding continuing to think I'm the only bad guy here."

Bob had a point. He'd been a prince to keep the secret. But I couldn't open my mouth and say words that I wasn't sure were true. I couldn't move any faster than I was moving, even knowing it would make things easier for him. We took our dilemma to a pastor we both respected. Gary listened carefully, said he understood the terrible timing, empathized with Bob, and at the same time understood that I just couldn't do what he was asking.

Monday before the wedding, Jim, Jonae, Mary, and I were at my dining-room table filling "welcome to our wedding weekend" bags they planned to put in each guest's hotel room. Jim said, "I've been thinking about you two, and I have some questions." Shoot, we said. Jim pulled out a little spiral pad and opened it. "I just want you to know where my thinking has been," he said. "You don't have to answer any of these." Jim had been living in Germany while these changes were going on in our lives, and clearly he'd been puzzling about it.

I don't remember most of the questions. One was about sex: "What do you do?" Another was about coming out. "Why do you have to tell anyone?" he asked. Mary, silent as I was while he read his list, could not let that one go unanswered.

"Coming out is always important," she said. "Coming out helps you get over whatever shame you may have felt, every time you put it into words. It's an act of love, sharing your most intimate self with another person. And coming out is always a chance to ask those you love if they can love you in this new reality."

As it happened, Bob's mother got sick and couldn't come to the wedding, but Ellen and Bill, my good friends and in-laws for more than thirty-five years, came. They enjoyed Mary when they met her at the Oktoberfest party for out-of-town guests on Friday of the wedding weekend. At the wedding, Tanene and I were escorted to the front of the church, where we sat with Jonae's grandmother; my sister, Jean, and her husband, Bob; Bob's sister, Ellen, and her husband, Bill. Bob, Katie, and Jonae's sister, Janelle, were in the wedding party. Mary, taking photographs of the bride's entry and the newlyweds' exit, sat in the back—with Pamela.

Bill Smith and I always kidded about being the "outlaws" of the Woodruff family, so it was fun when he asked me to dance at the reception. But then he confided in me, expecting, I'm sure, that I'd be delighted, that he had told Ellen that if they went to Bob's house, he would *not* go into the bedroom. I said to him, "You know, Bill, it took two of us to get here, it's not all Bob's fault." It wasn't much, but at least I made a stab at honestly acknowledging that I was as much to blame as Bob for our divorce. The cost of hiding the truth and asking friends and family to collude in the deception was a giant stomachache by the end of the evening.

On the morning of Jim's wedding, I looked at myself in the mirror and decided that my teeth were crooked, so I couldn't let them show in any of the official photographs made that day. Now I look at those photos and see the truth beneath the truth. Here was a woman who couldn't open her mouth all day, who silenced herself with fear and shame. And deeply wounded someone she loved, to boot.

Immediately after Jim and Jonae's wedding, I left for a trip to Cornwall with a few of my book-group friends, packing my silence and guilt in my carry-on suitcase. We stayed in a flat on a former manor house estate with Auntie Bubbles, the aunt of one of my friends. Day after day we hiked the Cornish coast path, eating ploughman's specials in pubs for lunch, clotted cream and scones for afternoon tea. When we visited St. Michael's Mount—a place that called to me because I had always envisioned my own angel as Michael—I bought a silver ring for myself, fashioned as a Celtic knot. The Celtic knot goes around and around, weaving back on itself, with no beginning and no end. It was the perfect metaphor for my inner conflict.

Chapter 23

MARY AND I MARKED the New Year's Eve after Jim and Jonae's wedding with nothing pleasant to anticipate in the New Year. We had come to a stuck place.

"I said I'd wait until it felt unhealthy to me," said Mary, "and I'm there. I need to let you go. If you don't find yourself, you'll never be able to find life with me."

Both of us knew she was right. We wrote a letter together and sent it to our family and friends in early January, announcing our decision to part and asking for support. Then we wished each other well and went our separate ways. It was agony. And it was right.

I had wrestled with the choice between Bob and Mary. Letting go of Bob—or being let go by Bob, as it were—I was free to choose Mary. And while my heart knew I was headed there, still I stalled. I was unable to move on and move in with her. Why? I had known for at least two years that the choice was not about trading one external authority (Bob) for another (Mary). The challenge was to find my own internal authority. Mary said that if I couldn't find myself, I would never find her. And she was right.

When I was a child, my mother was my authority. I could say my parents, perhaps, as it was a tossup between my mother's anger and my father's silence. Then, marrying when I did, I gave authority to my husband. And, as time went on, to the church. All those external authorities, and the terrorists in me making sure I paid attention to them, perhaps it is no wonder I was so slow to develop a sense of my own authority.

When I finally began to assert myself, I did so in awkward, "not nice" ways, and often got scared silent if anyone came back at me. I was used to being a Good girl, a Good woman, so used to acquiescing that I had no skill at holding my own in a calm, confident manner. It's not that I didn't have opinions; I did, especially about things I could back up with my intellect. But when it came to feelings, I was more adept at honoring those of others. I was a beginner at honoring my own, recognizing a gut instinct as truth for me, and acting on it.

It took landing in the hospital in October 1985 with a serious GI problem that was ultimately diagnosed as "diarrhea of unknown origin," for me to tip to the fact that the work environment and partnership expectations at Donworth-Taylor were becoming toxic for me. It took two more years and another hospital stay for me to get the clarity and courage to act on that information and leave to start Woodruff Associates. I had felt "home" in my guts the first day I went to Mary's, but five years later I still couldn't let go of the need to please everyone so I could do what I knew I wanted to do.

There was another thing. I lived most of my adult life as an extrovert, out there with people, taking my cues from them. A high need for inclusion meant that I wanted to be part of almost any group I was invited to join, and that I wanted to include as many people as possible in any circle of which I was a part. In a way, I continued the pattern set in high school of dashing between one activity or group and another. In the eighties and nineties, I was consulting more and more and at deeper and deeper levels, marveling at the privilege. I was writing and studying poetry, loving the poetry group that met once a month or so to write and share. I was an active Presbyterian elder. I mentored consultants-to-be in the OSR program, the Community Consulting Practicum and the Northwest Cluster. And I had three circles of women who were vital to me: the Gathering of Women, a spirit group, and the eight of us who've become like sisters.

Once I said to Bob, "It feels as though our home is like a gas station, where two very exhausted people drop in to get filled up in order to get right back out on the road again."

He said, "I see that. What's wrong with it?"

"I want home to be a destination," I responded. I yearned to settle into home, for home to hold as much richness for us as any of the other places in which we found so much satisfaction and meaning. Bob was mystified.

Now I understood myself to be an introvert. Poetry and voice dialogue were vehicles through which I began to hear my own voice in the nineties. They required quiet space. I began to claim that space out of near desperation then to welcome it as a refuge and a place of light. In that solitude, I could listen deep inside myself and begin to find me.

Still, habit was strong, obligations I had chosen to accept required fulfilling, and even the dance with Mary occupied so much time that time for myself seemed stolen and infrequent. I think one of the things I loved about my little rental house was that it provided me with sanctuary to sink into myself and do my own work.

When Mary and I suspended our relationship, I was utterly alone without a coupled future for the first time in my adult life. I waded into the great unknowing of winter, the season of water, holding all my questions, determined to honor the words of Lao Tzu in the *Tao Te Ching* that I had learned in SOPHIA:

Do you have the patience to wait
till your mud settles and the water is clear?
Can you remain unmoving
till the right action arises by itself?

>Lao-Tzu. *The Tao Te Ching: A New English Version.*
>Translated by Stephen Mitchell. Harper Collins, 1988.

Chapter 24

THAT JANUARY was as Januarys are in the Pacific Northwest: dark, cold, and rainy, with occasional periods of brilliant sunshine. I holed up in my little house at the top of the hill for the month, doing the consulting work I had scheduled, but otherwise seeing no one, nor answering phone calls except from my children.

On January 5, I sat in front of my computer, to write my first journal entry of the new year. I wrote down all my questions:

1. Can I love myself? And can I love myself enough as I am, whatever that "I am" is?

2. Do I believe God loves me? Did God create me? What does God have in mind for my life?

3. How will I reconcile myself with my anger with God?

4. Where does Bob fit in with my life—or not?

5. Am I going to be a woman who favors women for intimate relationship? And if so, will I choose Mary for a life partner—or not?

6. How will I deal with my homophobia?

This is a lot of introspection (I continued), and I have done a lot of it already. At the same time, I know I have avoided for months the very thing I need: enough quiet that I can truly settle into prayer, that I can *listen* for that still, small voice of truth to ring out for me.

I can't expect any individual to give me what I need to be giving myself—that sense that I am OK, that I have meaning, that I am lovable. That's why the first question is so important. Can I love myself? And why is it that I have trouble with that? I will not turn this question into a Bob-or-Mary issue. It is a Mary Ann question, a question for me—and God.

I sat quietly at my computer for several minutes, until something that seemed not to be my own voice came to me. Heart pounding, I inserted a table into my journal document on the screen and formatted it like a script. I typed:

God: Of course I love you. I've loved you from the moment you were conceived, even before that. How could you doubt my love for you?

Trembling at the audacity of this, I continued:

Me: God, I'm so confused. I don't even know what I think about you these days. Are you the God of Original Blessing or the God of Judgment?

God: I am neither, simply. And both, obviously. I am bigger than any person's ability to fence me in with descriptions.

Me: Help me, God.

God: I will. Listen for me. I am here for you all the time. I love you. I created you, how could I not love you? Be at peace. All will be known to you. You already know. Breathe. You are loved. Your only job is to love. I have sent you here to love, to learn how to love, to love a world that needs it badly.

Me: What about judgment?

God: There is enough judgment in the world. People judge all the time, as you know, because you do it and believe everyone is doing it of you. But there is only one judgment that really matters, and that is the final judgment, which is mine to make. Love, I tell you, love! That is what I want more of in this world, love. Help people to love, and you will be doing what I have asked of you. If you learn to love, *starting with yourself*, Mary Ann, you will have learned all I wanted you to know.

Thus began a dialogue that continued for eighty pages throughout that month. Each morning I would arise early, make a cup of coffee, and take it to my computer. I would look out at the bird feeder hanging from the tree outside. I watched chickadees and nuthatches feeding while a squirrel prowled along the split-rail fence across the drive, frustrated at the cage around the bird feeder that kept him off it. Then I would write. Many days I did nothing but write in that computer journal. On the days I had business to do, I would get up early and write first. I had to get this—me!—figured out. I had no Plan B.

Me: I wish I hadn't hurt anyone.

God: You haven't. You can't. You only have to follow your heart and decide which risks you are going to take and which not. The other people in your life are on their own path, making their own decisions and learning from the consequences. You can't hurt them by making honest choices and being honest about them. Not even I hurt people, Mary Ann, and I'm God, so don't get so big in your britches. People's hurts come from growth, which almost always involves risks and choices. The only way to avoid hurting is to stay in one place, and even that would hurt after a while.

Me: What I don't love is the part of me that's made my life so upside down—running back and back to Mary, ruining my marriage, scaring my children, making things difficult for my friends, my own fear choking me and keeping me from being able to live big enough...

God: Did I not say it is all about *love*? What have you done except follow love? Love as you experienced it, felt drawn toward it?

Me: Yeah, but what about not being faithful to Bob's love? He loved me, and I loved him. And I promised till death do us part, and then I broke that promise.

God: You and Bob had an agreement, a promise. To live together, to support each other, to love each other in sickness and in health, for better for worse, until death do you part. I don't take that lightly, and neither did either of you. You stuck together through some thick and thin, and you know it.

Me: You're not helping me feel any better here, God.

God: I don't know the answer, Mary Ann, not totally. You both grew, and life took you in some different directions, directions that the love between you couldn't embrace. If you want me to say that you were getting ready for the bigger challenge of loving a woman and what that might mean, I'm not sure I can say that. I don't dole things out like that. I am everywhere, simply sending love and wanting love to reign. I saw the challenge unfold for you, and I have been with you every step of the way. Could you and Bob have stayed in friendship if I hadn't?

I poured everything into the dialogues with God. Day after day I carried on these morning "conversations," typing furiously, capturing what I "heard" God say to me. My heart raced right along with my fingers.

Me: I think I'm not over the divorce. Do you ever get over a divorce? Get over—what does that mean? Is divorce a hurdle you have to jump over? So that you can get it behind you?

God: What does the divorce mean to you?

Me: It means a failure. A disappointment because we won't be together for the rest of our lives, renting a house in Hawaii where we and all our children and grandchildren celebrate our fiftieth anniversary.

It's also a loss of Bob. The character he is, the widely interested person he is, the optimist, the full-hearted person he is, the struggling-to-grow, even-to-be-quiet-occasionally person he is. I really miss all those parts of Bob as a person. And the divorce means that he will share those parts of himself not with me but with others, including someone who will ultimately be his wife—because he really wants to be married.

There's another piece too. I'm a beginner at being around Bob when he isn't with me. I am a beginner at being in a room when his energy strides into it. I am a beginner at holding my own energy quiet and calm, hearing his big voice, his big laugh, feeling the room fill up with Bob, fighting not to get small myself in comparison.

You are really quiet, God. I cannot even imagine what you might be thinking. I guess I'd love to hear you say that you understand, that this is just a phase, and that I'll get through it, or over it.

God: Well, the truth is, I love Bob. I am totally tickled that he is in my world, that his spirit is out there for people to hear, feel, see.

Me: I knew you'd feel that way. I thought about that yesterday. How happy you must be to have a Bob Woodruff in your world.

God: He has a unique gift to give, and he gives it unreservedly.

And I am totally delighted that you are in my world, too. I'm only saying this because you are practically begging me to say it. It really goes without saying. Everything that I have created is good.

Me: Ted Kaczynski? [1]

God: Don't distract me. Let's just sit here awhile with your jealousy and envy. I will be with you here. I think your jealousy and envy really come out of a hurt place...right?

Me: Of course. I am hurt because Bob wouldn't listen to me, because he had to have his own way and couldn't hear mine. I am hurt because so much of the time, I couldn't get clear enough fast enough, so I couldn't even speak up for something other than what he wanted. I just fought against it, because it was his idea. I think I am hurt because I was practically invisible to both of us, mainly me. I wish Bob could have said, as Mary has, I'm not going anywhere; I love you and will stay here while you do whatever you need to do.

God: And he didn't.

Me: No. He said, "Play me or trade me." He ran out of patience, because my process was so slow.

God: All Bob did was ask you, listen between the lines to your responses—because you didn't or couldn't say much straight out—and then decide to take action since you weren't about to.

Me: You're right. God, I want to be bigger than jealousy and envy. I want to be bigger than fear and paralysis, too. Will you help me?

---

[1] Ted Kaczynski, known as the Unabomber, was a recluse whose homemade bombs, mailed or hand-delivered, had killed three persons and wounded many others between 1978 and 1996, when he was finally arrested in a remote Montana cabin.

God: Of course, Mary Ann. I love you and am always here to help you. You are precious, lovable—and don't you ever forget it.

Sunday, January 11, I woke early in the morning with a dream of sex that was so profound it shook me to the core and left me with only the words *oh God oh God oh God*.

God: Yes, my child, yes.

Me: And God, to you also, yes. Yes. Yes to the gift you have given me, the profound gift. Yes to your love, yes to being your love as best I can be in the world. Yes to my life.

God: Yes. Yes to you, my child, yes to you.

This is extraordinary, I write in my journal. I leave this prayer with the idea that I must go for a walk. I dress in my sweats, turtleneck, red down jacket. It is cold, thirty-four on the thermometer. I walk toward the north end of the island along the winding road of East Mercer Way. The firs and hemlocks are fragrant in the icy air.

I stop at the parkway that opens out after the trees. In the distance Mount Baker is shimmering in the sunlight of the north Cascades, a sliver of brilliance between the horizon and a low band of dark clouds heavy with the next rain shower.

"Hello, Mount Baker," I say aloud, "I'm gay." I shut my eyes, waiting for the volcano to erupt. When I look again it is simply standing there, radiant in the sun. "Hey, Mount Baker," I call, a bit louder, "I'm a lesbian." Mount Baker gleams back, a shining witness. I feel a stone drop inside me into a deep pool—of calmness.

Thank you, God, I think in amazement. Thank you for waking me up at 5:25 this morning so I could make this discovery, thank you for the clear, clear message, right to my core, thank you. I breathe. I keep looking at Mount Baker. The mountain beams back at me.

Standing there, I imagine talking to Bob. I love you, Bob, and always will. For all we've shared and all we have to share in the future—children, grandchildren—destiny has brought us together, and I am so grateful. I love you for having said what you said way back: "If this is the way you want to go with your life, Mary Ann, I'll support you and you'll never hear a bad word from me about it." What a gift that is. I need your support. I'll always have a jealous part of me that thinks life will go easier for you…but then I stop myself. Why wouldn't life go easier for me if I am easier with who I am? I've come to realize, I continue in my imaginary conversation with Bob, that my deepest intimacy will be with a woman, and I am going to ask Mary to consider sharing life with me. I want you to be the first to know.

Or maybe second to Jim and Katie. I imagine asking Jim and Jonae if they are free next Saturday night and if I can come spend the evening with them in Portland. I imagine asking them if I can invite Katie, too. Then I would talk to them all together. Tell them where I have arrived and ask them for their support.

I imagine taking a dozen long stemmed yellow roses to Mary with a card that says YES.

I walk back home, deep in gratitude. I stay quiet, by myself, holding this new knowing to my heart, living into the ramifications.

Several days later, I wrote:

> **Me:** God, while I was walking this morning you told me that Mary is an angel sent to teach me compassion, beauty and—what was the other thing?—oh, yes, courage.

God: That's right. Oh, Mary Ann, do you have any idea how I delight in Mary Dispenza?

Me: God, is there anyone you don't delight in?

God: Does a gardener not delight in all the flowers and variety of foliage, all the colors and shapes and textures in her garden? Of course I delight in all my creation—for the most part.

Me: Ted Kaczynski again...

God: You put him in there, not I. What I meant is that there certainly are times when people act in ways I wish they wouldn't. But mainly, yes, I delight in all my creatures. Just look at you watching those dear little birds outside your window. Do you relish the nuthatches more than the chickadees?

Me: No, nor do I enjoy more the towhees or juncos or pine siskins—although I would love to see more pine siskins; they are certainly making themselves rare this winter.

God: Rarity is one of the things that increase the sense of delight. And Mary delights me for just that reason, she is so rare.

Me: Indeed she is. God, last night I began reading Mary's book by Rob Eichberg, *Coming Out; an Act of Love*. And I got frightened, reading the stories of people in the book: the years of self-hate and fear and feeling that their parents would throw them out or disown them, all those inner tapes of sicko, pervert, queer, dyke... it scares me so, God,

I don't know what to do. I wish I didn't have to own any of this. Didn't have to tell anyone, could go back and pretend or... or *hide*! Help!

God: You know those voices are in the world. I won't pretend they aren't, Mary Ann. I wish they weren't. What I want you to know is this is perfectly all right with me.

Me: What "this" is perfectly all right with you?

God: This love. Desiring a woman.

Me: It's all right with you?

God: Of course.

Me: You are very sure?

God: Yes, I am very sure.

Me: I'm not just making this up because it feels better to me?

God: Mary Ann, dear heart, listen to me. *All that matters is love!* That's all I ever had in mind. It's all I have in mind now.

Me: Then God, why are so many people so certain that it is an abomination?

God: It's that Old Testament. I knew we'd be in trouble when people canonized it. That was then, this is now.

Me: ...Do you forgive me—for falling in love with Mary while I was still married, for the divorce, for all of it?

God: I say that you ought to forgive yourself. The final judgment is in my hands and is not yours to know. Leave it with me. Lugging a bag full of guilt and regret will make it hard for you to move with ease for the rest of your life, and I need your energy unimpeded. I need you for good in the world. Humility is a good thing—so you understand that you are not perfect. But paralyzing guilt is not required. Confess—you have done that—and then let it go. I love you. Now—on your way rejoicing.

Me: Oh, God, oh, God, thank you. Thank you, thank you.

God: You are welcome. You are well come.

Bible Story

> This feller jumped Old Jacob,
> wanted to fight with him real bad,
> wrapped him up in steel arms like barrel bands,
> straddled his shoulders to squeeze the breath out of him,
> tied his legs in knots until his knees screamed,
> wanted to hear Old Jacob whimper "uncle."
>
> Who woulda blamed Jacob for caving in?
> *Who asked me to be a hero*, he wondered,
> wriggling there in the dust, his head down,
> trying to figure it out,
> this guy outta nowhere.

It was a rough night for Old Jacob,
tired already from his journey and all,
no rest, not even a stone to lay his head on,
just this nutty lunatic all over him
like he had six legs and a dozen arms,
and all of them bent on grinding Jacob into sand.

But you know? Old Jacob was a wily guy himself,
determined as hell when his dander got up.
He grabbed that feller, rolled over on him
got him in a hammer lock and wouldn't budge,
even when the feller begged him to.
No, he said, *not until you bless me.*

Come the dawn,
durned if that feller didn't bless Old Jacob,
gave him the territory,
a new name even,
and they parted friends.

That Bible sure has some crazy stories, doesn't it?

Coming Out

Chapter 25

I CALLED JIM and Jonae to ask if they could have visitors the weekend of January 17 and 18, and I went to Portland to be with them. Katie joined us from California. They were all gentle with me, waiting for me to get around to what I wanted to say. I was so nervous about how they would react that I put it off and put it off, savoring their company, not wanting to break the magic. When I finally got the words out on Sunday, Katie, for one, was relieved. She thought I'd called them together to tell them I had cancer. As for my love for Mary, she'd had me figured out long ago and was just glad I'd come to myself.

Jim said, "I'm amazed that you moved so fast," and Katie added, "or so slowly, as the case may be."

I laughed and said, "Five years." Exhaling.

Though divorced parents imagine their children always harbor the hope they will get back together, Jim and Katie were clear that the idea of our remarrying was a fairy tale. Jim said that Bob and I had moved in such different directions that he couldn't even support the notion of our getting back together. It surprised me that none of the three wanted it or thought it was possible.

Holding the space of being not married but loving friends is so much better than hating each other or not being able to stand being in the same room together. I love Bob like my own skin, I told Jim,

Katie, and Jonae; he feels that close. He is fun, exuberant, intelligent, and has taught me a lot of things I would never have learned if I'd stayed a Sparklin. I love him like a brother, I said. I can even feel the sibling rivalry with him.

That weekend gave me the opportunity to grieve with my kids the real end of my marriage, although it seems the kids had done that long ago. But I needed to do it, and I needed to do it with them. It was a chance for me to tell three people who mean the world to me the Mount Baker story and what had happened for me in the last two weeks. I wanted to give them a chance to tell me how it felt for them, invite them to ask questions, share feelings, whatever. They gave me their blessing.

A week later, I met with Bob. We walked the path at Seattle's Lincoln Park along Puget Sound. Ferries went back and forth from the mainland to Vashon Island as we talked. When we got back to our cars, we drove up to a little neighborhood café for dinner. It was an easy time, a calm, honest time. I told him the story of my January so far, and he listened seriously, saying, "Good for you."

At dinner he said, "I'm sorry we won't grow old together," and I told him of the fantasy I had held that we would remarry, that when we took everyone to Hawaii to celebrate our fiftieth, we would laugh at the fact that we'd only really been married forty-seven years. We both acknowledged that we mattered that much to each other. I said, "We *can* grow old together, Bob... It'll be in another form, and there will be others along with us." The whole evening felt like a blessing, and I went home in peace.

The next day I had a message on my phone from Bob. "You did a good job yesterday," he said, "and I thought I did a good job, too, walking around and around together, listening. And I went home and thought, 'I feel OK about this.' Then at 1:30 in the morning I sat upright in bed and asked myself, 'What is going on here? What's wrong?' and I realized it is the finality of it—and I have a lot of grief about that. I'll be OK with it, I'll take care of myself in it, I just wanted to say that."

That felt real to me. There *is* grief with this, I thought, and we'd be foolish to pretend otherwise. I appreciated Bob's letting me know. Another blessing.

Saturday, January 31, I spent with Mary. I took over a bouquet of yellow sweetheart roses and baby's breath, with a card marked, YES. Inside I wrote, "Yes, Mary, yes, yes with all my heart, yes." I held her and wept, noting the profound relief it was to be there with a yes. There were few words. She showed me around her house. She had spent the month cleaning out—closets, papers, chapters in her life that no longer served her, throwing away clothes, giving them to Goodwill. She had straightened up her office, too. And there on her drafting table was a framed piece of art she had done for me, a rainbow of water colors, and against it these words: "Oh God, within the body of Ruth Ann Sparklin nothing about me from beginning to end was hid from *your* eyes. How frightfully, fantastically wonderful it all is." The words from my favorite psalm, 139, taken from a book I had loaned her, *Psalms Now*. Knowing what I had to tell her, seeing those words, I wept again. How did she know to do that? What a mystery is this spiritual connection we have, I thought. Still I listened to her, wanting to let her talk first.

She had applied for a new job she would truly love to have. She had refinanced her home and rid herself of credit card debt. She had been reading a book on solitude and was full of what the book said about the need for solitude as well as connection in relationship. Again I thought, what a miracle! That is what I have discovered I need—solitude. And without solitude I can't have any relationship that won't eat me alive. I was struck by the wonder before me, this gentle woman, strong spirit, lovingly putting before me the very things I would need to move forward in life with her.

Then we got into my car and left her house. We walked Lincoln Park—walked and talked. I told her about my month. Now that I am writing this I see that we were both doing the very same work: taking care of the things that needed to be attended to in order for us to move forward in life, together or not. She in an external, tangible way, I in an internal, intangible way. I, too, had cleaned out my (internal) closets and come to terms with parts of my life that no longer served. She had strengthened her financial position and was standing on more solid ground in a material sense. And I had found myself and stood on more solid ground, too, a better balance of ego and self.

When we sat on a rock by Alki Beach after lunch, Mary peppered me with questions. "Well, what about us?" she said. "I need to hear not just that you have come to peace about your sexual orientation. I want to hear that you are excited to move forward in partnership with me, that you're ready to do that. Not necessarily move in together, but just move forward. Are you ready for that? And are you willing to tell people that you are really excited to do that, now that you have found yourself?"

I wanted to give an honest answer. I wanted to savor this new understanding of myself, really ground myself in this experience of coming out, I told her. I didn't want to rush, to diffuse the sense of mystery, the deep joy of settling into this peace. I needed to walk with the wonder of this arrival for a while, this place of coming to myself. And then certainly, I told Mary, now that I have a me to bring to a partnership, let's begin to see how that will be.

And so we did.

Chapter 26

HAVING MARRIED originally with the romantic notion that Bob and I were two halves that would somehow make a whole, it was crucial to me, now that I had a stronger sense of my own self, for Mary and me to have a partnership that honored us as whole individuals. She was fully in agreement, as she had said so often.

With freedom to love and without role expectations, we crafted a spaciousness that continues to astound me. Moments of amazing intimacy are interspersed with respect for our separateness. We protect each other's solitude and delight in each other's company. It is almost as if we are those two young sixth graders at times, up the same tree, yet resting on our own branches. We are worthy opponents as partners, too; we have abundant opportunities to practice how to disagree, to stay present, and to hold our own in calmness. Mary's early pattern of disappearing emotionally when things get tough, and my early pattern of assuming any emotionally loaded situation is my fault, have provided us with plenty of fodder for growth.

I turned sixty in June 1998. Mary and friends helped me give my own party on the lawn of my sanctuary home. It was a beautiful, sunny day, and my friends wore crazy hats to reflect my theme of outrageousness. My friend Marian, who was always in hats or scarves those days because of chemotherapy, and for whose comfort I had come up with the idea of hats, arrived at the party with her bald head tattooed by her grandson. Katie flew up from California, bringing a zillion words on Post-it notes which she spread all over the outside of my living room window wall. People rearranged them to create poems as gifts to me. We ate cracked crab and strawberry shortcake. Jim and Jonae were there, too, as were Bob and Pamela, she briefly, on her way to the airport. At some point, Bob, Mary, Jim, Katie, Jonae, and I posed for a picture, our arms around each other, each in a silly hat. This is our family now, I thought. That's really outrageous. And fabulous.

In December 1998, I moved into Mary's house for what we called the Great Experiment. I continued to pay rent on my little house for six months—my backup plan, just in case.

It was wonderful living together. No more back and forth, just the simple joy of being under the same roof, waking up together, shaping a life that was ours. We gave a Light Party that December, a Christmas/solstice celebration that's become a tradition to this day. It's our opportunity to gather with friends to affirm love, friendship, and the promise that "the light shines in the darkness and the darkness cannot put it out."

In spring 2000, we purchased a house that was new to both of us. We were having some work done on it before we moved in, so when Mary said we needed to drop an extension cord off for the workmen on the way to my birthday dinner on June 6, I didn't suspect a thing. But when we drove up the driveway, I could hear music coming from the house.

"Want to come in?" asked Mary, her eyes twinkling. We walked in to a cellist and violinist playing chamber music in our empty, high-ceilinged living room. A card table was set for two before the fireplace, candles glowing, and from the kitchen came the aroma of dinner cooking.

"Happy birthday!" said the caterer, handing us glasses of champagne. We settled down by the fireplace, bathed in music and romance, and toasted each other: "Home."

Gratitude

I wonder.
Does a tree trunk thank the leaves
for shading her roots, for the miracle
of photosynthesis that gives her life?
Does the horizon thank the sky
for painting benediction to each evening,
streaking his hills with crimson gold?

I wonder,
Does a footpath thank the feet
whose determined passing keeps it open?
Do flat stones
thank the children who skip them on the rim
of the lake, do those stones shout
joy at unexpected lightness?

I wonder,
Does breath thank laughter
for giving it voice, shaking loose its ribbed prison?
Does a honeycomb thank the bee who fills it?
Does the heart, in the dark where no one hears,

whisper thank you to mind body soul
for the song it sings?

I wonder,
Does the beach thank the ocean when,
after pounding and rolling with the storm
it runs its fingers gently up her back,
easing the knots and ripples raised by wind,
draws her softly down to the edge where,
in the foam and running sanderlings,
they rest together,
ebb and flow.

I wonder.

Chapter 27

PEOPLE MIGHT SAY the most difficult part of the spiritual journey is going into that deep, deep place to find the pearl of great price, one's self. For me, the even greater challenge was bringing myself up and out into the light.

When I told my sister, Jean, early on about my feelings for Mary, she gave me a big hug and declared, "There is so little love in the world, we should celebrate it wherever it shows up." I would crawl from here to Hartford to help her anytime she needs me, in gratitude for that instant affirmation and acceptance.

Coming Out, An Act of Love, Rob Eichberg's book, speaks of coming out on three levels: personal, private, and public.

The personal level I knew from the plunge of January 1998, the days and voice dialogues with God that culminated in what I call my Mount Baker moment. I emerged from that time at peace with the mystery, the wonder, of my life. Now I knew and accepted that I had a gay part to acknowledge. That was my personal coming out. All the support of my family and friends as I wrestled with my life, while incredibly important, couldn't have gotten me there. I had to do it alone to know it was real.

The private level of coming out began with my weekend in Portland with my children, included my walk and dinner with Bob, my taking flowers and the YES card to Mary's. There were many dinners in my house that spring, gatherings in which I told my story to groups of friends who had been supportive all along the way, and who I thought deserved to know where I had arrived. Some of those friends were gays or lesbians who understood fully the implications of my yes, and were ready to stand by with support as I enlarged the circle.

The public level of coming out was gradual and depended on my assessments of risk and trust. At Easter 1998, I wrote to my Christmas card list of friends and family about Mary. For my fortieth college reunion in 2000, I included Mary in my profile for the class book, and sent the outrageous photo of our "new" family taken at my sixtieth birthday party. I had many responses, none that were not written in love.

The biggest barrier to total openness about my new reality was the church. It was the church that presented the greatest possibility for rejection.

The Presbyterian Church (USA) is governed by a constitution established in 1983, at the time the United Presbyterian Church merged with the Southern Presbyterian Church in the United States. Part I of the constitution is the *Book of Confessions*, setting out the creeds by which the church expresses its beliefs. Part II is the *Book of Order*, which defines rules for governance, worship, and discipline. A part of the *Book of Order*, known informally as Amendment B (actually G-6.0106.b), has created controversy in the church for years. It reads:

> *Those who are called to office in the church are to lead a life in obedience to Scripture and in conformity to the historic confessional standards of the church. Among these standards is the requirement to live either in fidelity within the covenant of mar-*

riage between a man and a woman (W-4.9001), or chastity in singleness. Persons refusing to repent of any self-acknowledged practice which the confessions call sin shall not be ordained and/or installed as deacons, elders, or ministers of the Word and Sacrament.

It is Amendment B that gave me such a stomachache. Amendment B put me at odds with some good Presbyterians with whom I had served. Amendment B said I couldn't be what I had been, an ordained elder in the church. Amendment B sent me away from Mercer Island Presbyterian Church, while I worked to come to terms with myself. And though in 2000, I joined a new Presbyterian church, Newport, where the ministers were supportive, Amendment B continued to haunt me.

In 2001, the Presbyterian Church was going through yet another attempt to amend the *Book of Order* and liberalize the standards for ordination. At the annual general assembly in 2000, an Amendment A had been passed which, if approved, would allow single gay persons or those in committed relationships to be ordained and serve as deacons, elders, or "ministers of the Word and Sacrament." Any amendment passed at the general assembly requires a majority of presbyteries in the country to vote to approve it. The vote on Amendment A in the presbytery of Seattle was approaching.

Each church sends to presbytery its ordained pastors and an equal number of elders from the session as delegates. The delegates are not instructed by session, but vote their own consciences. Still, most sessions discuss controversial issues, both to become informed and to allow for a sense of the session to develop. When the pastors of Newport Presbyterian Church asked me to speak to the session about the impact of Amendment B on me, I was uneasy. Trusting them, though, I accepted.

The evening arrived. I could feel a pulse throbbing in my throat as I entered the session room and sat down. Gary Schwab, the senior pastor, introduced me. I began.

> "I want to start with Psalm 139. I'm reading from the book, *Psalms/Now*, my companion since 1973, words by Leslie Brandt. This is the psalm that begins, 'O God, You know me inside and out, through and through.' Here is the part I want to read:
>
> *There is no way to escape You, no place to hide.*
> *If I ascend to the heights of joy,*
>   *You are there before me.*
> *If I am plunged into the depths of despair,*
>   *You are there to meet me.*
> *I could fly to the other side of our world*
>   *and find You there to lead the way.*
> *I could walk into the darkest of nights,*
>   *only to find You there*
>   *to lighten its dismal hours.*
>
> *You were present at my very conception.*
> *You guided the molding of my unformed members*
>   *within the body of my mother.*
> *Nothing about me, from beginning to end,*
>   *was hid from Your eyes.*
> *How frightfully, fantastically wonderful it all is!*

May Your all-knowing, everywhere-present Spirit
> *continue to search out my feelings and thoughts.*
Deliver me
>> *from that which may hurt or destroy me,*
>> *and guide me along the paths of love and truth.*

I looked around the table. Some of the faces belonged to friends; some were people I didn't even know. Every face was solemn. My voice threatened to desert me as I continued.

"I met Mary nearly nine years ago. In spite of feeling a practically instant sense of 'home,' it would be more than five years before I could say yes to that call. A lot of that was because of the church.

"I struggled, of course, with what God might think. The fundamentalist voices are strong in me, and I had to do diligence on the scriptures, which I did. But it killed me to know that some people in the church—who had been friends and colleagues, who thought I was pretty much OK and had something to contribute—would instantly consider me beyond the pale if they knew this one additional part of me. And, to be honest, I was one of those people myself. I didn't want this part. This is not how I imagined my life would go.

"At one point, I left the Presbyterian Church, because I could not come to grips with my own inner voices in the midst of the clamor of the official church's wrangling. I left the church, but never God. Oh, I was in constant communication with God—arguing, pleading—'Why me? Why this? Why this now? What does this mean? I can't, I won't, I don't.' Finally, I cut off all contact with everyone, and I spent all of January 1998 in the quiet of my little house, alone. I stopped nagging God and promised to listen. I listened and listened. What I got back was some version of this: I created you, Mary Ann. I have always loved you. I want you. I need you. As you.

"It was sort of like:

> *I was present at your very conception.*
> *I guided the molding of your unformed members*
>   *within the body of your mother.*
> *Nothing about you, from beginning to end,*
>   *was hid from My eyes.*

"I made a commitment from that moment to live my life to the best of my ability on the path of love and truth, trusting God for guidance. I choose, every day, to live from a place of love rather than a place of fear. And some days, that's work. That's why I am willing to talk to you tonight, although I would like to act as though these *Book of Order* issues have been settled or at least are not very important."

My hands shook a bit as I peeled off page after page of my written notes, stacking them to my side.

"You ask how Amendment B affects me. I will give you one specific example. About a month ago, I was called by the chair of the presbytery's nominating committee and asked to consider accepting a nomination to be on the presbytery's personnel committee. There it was, the moment I'd speculated about, when I had to face the reality of the mismatch between my church and me. It helped that the personnel committee did not particularly appeal to me. But it threw me into the calculus that any gay person will describe: How do I handle this situation? Do I tell the truth about my life? And what happens if I do? Shall I give in to my fears? Shall I just say I'm too busy? What I said was, 'Joyce, I can't do this.'

"'Why?' she asked.

"'Because the church won't let me,' I replied, 'because of my life.'

"'I know,' she said.

"She knew! And still she asked me. She said the nominating committee believed I would be good in the position. 'But,' she added, 'I have to tell you that if you stand, your nomination is likely to be challenged on the floor of presbytery.' She said that she wished it were different, and I know, because I know her, that she meant it. It was only later that I realized what was missing. What was missing was a message that could have sounded like this: 'We believe this is a ruling that needs to be challenged, and we believe the way to do it is to put forth a credible candidate so we can personalize this issue. You'll be challenged on the floor of presbytery, but we will stand with you, and here's who the 'we' are.' Instead, the message I was left with was, 'We'd love to have you, but if you want to go for it, you're on your own.'"Well, I don't want to go for it, and I don't tell you this story because I am sad to be excluded from sitting on another presbytery committee. I've been an elder since the seventies and have had the privilege of serving with wonderful people on a variety of presbytery committees and commissions.

"The real point here is the hit on the way I feel about myself. Most days I can come to Newport, worship, play handbells, and serve and feel the love of God. I try not to think too much about the *Book of Order*. I voted against Amendment B as a commissioner from Mercer Island Presbyterian Church in 1997, keeping my own angst, confusion, and terror to myself. My sister was moderator of the presbytery of Southern New England when they voted against B last year. Her daughter, Barbara Hager, a Princeton Seminary graduate and ordained Presbyterian minister, is one of the advocates this time for Amendment A. Her name is in the credits of the video we watched a couple of weeks ago. Where I stand on A should be no surprise. But I would have supported A long before I met Mary Dispenza."

It was utterly still at that table in the session room. I met the somber eyes of Heidi Calhoun, the associate pastor. Heidi has a gay brother whose church future is as affected by this issue as mine.

I took a breath and moved on.

"Years ago, I wandered into the sanctuary of Mercer Island Presbyterian to pray late one afternoon, and inadvertently came upon our minister and one of my fellow session members sitting on the steps to the chancel, deep in earnest conversation. Somehow, intuitively, I knew what that was all about. We were then in the midst of the eighties Presbyterian church debate over the ordination of gays and lesbians. In that instant I got it that this man, my friend, was gay. He had never said a word. I observed his discomfort while we talked about the issue in session, and shortly after that he drifted away from the church. A few years later, I saw him singing in the Seattle Men's Chorus and had a chance to talk to him in the foyer. Then he died, of AIDS. It grieves me to know how the church, and I as a silent but suspecting accomplice, let him down when he was struggling with his life. Our ambiguity about sexuality, our willingness to say one's sexuality is, like all of our life, a gift from God, but *his* might be an abomination, sent him out into those dark nights. I do not think for a minute he lost touch with God. Indeed, if he is like most of the gay and lesbian persons I have met, he was in closer touch with God, and more clear about his need for God's grace and comfort, than many of us who show up in church every Sunday.

"It seems to me that the number one effect of Amendment B is a temptation to sacrilege: to profane something that is sacred. My life, your life, all our lives are sacred. I do not understand all of the mystery of my life, but I accept that it is a sacred gift from God, and I yearn for the church to affirm that."

I could hear the crack in my voice. I paused for another breath and continued.

"The second effect of Amendment B for me is sorrow. The official church's message, "Come, be part of us, you are welcome, *but* you are unworthy to be leaders of our people" is often received as: *You* are unworthy. I know you don't mean it, but that is what is heard. Through Mary, I have come to know many wonderful gay, lesbian, bisexual, and transgendered men and women, deeply spiritual persons who long for communion and community and cannot find it in the church we claim to be the body of Christ, because the church cannot embrace all of who they are. This rejection, and how it makes people reject themselves, makes me very, very sad. It even makes me wonder how long I can stay in the church.

"The final effect of Amendment B for me is chagrin. I am dismayed that the Presbyterian church is squandering its moral and spiritual capital on this issue, when there are homeless persons to be sheltered, hungry children to be fed, love to be experienced and expanded, so that all of God's people can live together in peace and harmony as our Creator intended.

"None of this negates my appreciation for or my commitment to Newport. These are painful matters. Thank you for listening."

It was utterly still in the room. I looked around the table. Some elders were looking down; the eyes that met mine were grave, some moist. Gary cleared his throat and thanked me for coming. I gathered my papers, pushed back my chair, stood up, and walked from the room.

* * *

In January 2002, the presbytery of Seattle met to vote. The motion that came to the floor recommended defeating Amendment A, the proposal that would have lifted the restrictions on ordination. The wording of the motion itself was a clue to where the presbytery was headed. I was asked to be one of four speaking in opposition to the motion. After days of reflection, I said yes. If I had any credibility with the members of presbytery, many of whom I had served with over the years, this might be the time to call on it. I hoped some people might say, "Well, if we are talking about people like Mary Ann Woodruff, we may need to change our minds."

The atmosphere was charged in the sanctuary of John Knox Presbyterian Church the evening of January 15. I was the last of four speakers for A, balanced by the pastor of the largest church in the presbytery, who spoke against it. One of my former pastors at Mercer Island was speaking against A as well. When it was my turn, I looked at the three friends who had come with me, took a deep breath, and stepped to the microphone. "My name is Mary Ann Woodruff," I said. "I am a member of Newport Presbyterian Church." I continued with my two-minute statement, excerpting from what I'd told the session of Newport.

The presbytery voted to uphold Amendment B, and I went home, crushed.

In March, I wrote to the session of Newport asking that my name be withdrawn from the membership rolls of the church. I told them, "By withdrawing from your membership rolls, I expect you to take my name off the list from which Newport pays its per capita portion to the larger church. I do not want any more money to go forward in support of the institutional church in my name. I want the Presbyterian Church (USA) to experience a drop in membership (even of one) and to have to grapple with the consequences of its decisions. This action is important to me as a matter of personal integrity. Count on me to continue as a 'friend of Newport,' supporting the work and ministry of this church as I can."

I was now totally *out*, living from my own inner authority and speaking for myself.

Say Nothing

What to say about the church?
Say it betrays me.
Say the Pharisees are winning the battle,
say narrowness and fear have taken captive
the followers of the Lord of Love.
Say the church has lost its heart,
say its moral beacon pierces with cold light,
makes life a harsh and colorless choice
between glare and shadow.
Say the church is a family
squabbling over power and control,
say the elder brothers refuse to attend the party
if the prodigals are coming.

What to say about the church?
Say God is still in charge
and—patiently or powerfully—
will win this war.

What to say about my rage?
Say nothing.

Chapter 28

IT WAS HOT IN THE EAST BAY of San Francisco the weekend of September 11–14, 2003. Really hot. The Bancroft Hotel in Berkeley had no air conditioning. It was Katie and Tim's wedding weekend.

Thursday night the Woodruff and Miller families got together for dinner, playing a game that Katie and Tim had created to see who knew the bride and groom the best. Tim has three brothers, all married, and delightful parents, Elone and Norm, who have been divorced for years. Tim's brother Ron was his best man, Tim's other brothers and Jim were to be ushers at the wedding; Katie's best friend, Cat, was her only attendant.

On Friday there was a picnic in a park for all the out-of-town family and friends and their children. Mary wowed the kids with her volleyball prowess, while I sat on a blanket visiting with my sister, Jean, her husband, Bob, friends Addi Brooks and Bob Pennell from Seattle, and Bob and Glenda, the woman he married in 2001.

Saturday was the wedding, at the Montclair Women's Cultural Arts Club in Oakland (sans air conditioning), with dinner and dancing following the ceremony.

Mary and I were escorted to the front row, as were Glenda, Jonae (carrying Rita Jo, our nine-month-old granddaughter), Elone, Tim's sisters-in-law, and Norm and Bonnie, Norm's companion. Bob brought Katie down the aisle to "Let's Do It" sung by the UC Berkeley Alumni Chorus, the group where Tim and Katie met. The wedding ceremony was a real look into Tim and Katie's hearts. They had each written five endings to the sentence that began, "I want to marry you because…" They read those to each other during the ceremony, hearing each other's statements for the first time, first one from Tim, then one from Katie. They laughed, they cried, and so did their guests. It was one of the most intimate weddings I have ever witnessed.

Photos and champagne followed the wedding. The family pictures were easy, all of us with broad smiles if shiny faces. At dinner, Mary and I were seated with my sister and her husband, our friends Carol Kelly and David Meekhof from Seattle, and Norm and Bonnie. When it was time to dance, we all danced, joining in the exuberance of the congo line and "YMCA" with family and Katie and Tim's clan of friends who know each other well and were ready to celebrate. Everyone welcomed us into the dance circles, dancing with both of us easily. Mary and I danced together, both Mary and I got Norm Miller onto the dance floor for a spin, and I danced "K-K-K-Katie" with Bob, a remembrance of our first night out after she was born. It was a joyous occasion. At the end of the evening, as the wedding planner and all of us parents were carrying things to the cars, Norm said to Mary and me, "You two are really nice." The hint of surprise in his voice said volumes.

What a difference there was between my experience of Jim's and Katie's weddings. It had nothing to do with the bride and groom, the rituals, the setting, or the friends. It had everything to do with where I was with myself, where Mary and I were, and where all of us were as a family. Together. Thank God.

Epilogue

IT IS AFTERNOON in Olympia, Washington, Wednesday, February 1, 2012. Two o'clock, to be exact. Mary and I are early. We drove an hour south from Bellevue, where we live, parked on the State Capitol Campus, and walked to the Legislative Building. Inside the building we climb three flights of marble steps, marveling at the five-ton Tiffany chandelier—said to be the largest ever made—hanging from the top of the Capitol's rotunda. "Let there be light," we breathe.

Reaching the third floor, we walk down the quiet hall and enter the senate chamber gallery. The senate chamber is empty and the gallery—actually two galleries, balconies on either side of the vaulted-ceilinged room and overlooking the chamber below—are nearly so. Only a guard and a few other early arrivals are there. We take our seats, hearts pounding. History is in the making today. Today the Washington State Senate is expected to pass a bill guaranteeing marriage equality to same-sex couples, a bill that will easily pass the House and that the governor has promised to sign into law.

We were early on July 23, 2007, too. We were the fourth couple in line at the office of the secretary of state in Olympia that morning, the first day it was possible to register as domestic partners in our state. We exited the building waving yellow roses to the crowd waiting in line for their turn; we had our picture taken next to a balloon-festooned convertible at the curb bearing a sign that read, Just Registered. We loved the idea of being "domesticated." Mary and I were surprised how moved we were by such simple acts as sitting at a window filling out forms saying we intended to be together forever and receiving a card and certificate from the state acknowledging our commitment.

Since 2007, marriage has been a hot topic in our home. Mary, ever the activist, has been all for our getting married. She sees it as an idea whose time has come. I have said, "Why get married when our own state wouldn't recognize it? Why get married when we wouldn't have any more rights than we have now under the state's domestic partnership law? When the federal government says we can file income taxes jointly or have the same rights of inheritance as other married couples, then I can see getting married." Mary has argued back that separate is not equal. She says our being married is important for our grandchildren.

Before Christmas last year I'd been reading *In Search of Belief*, a contemporary analysis of the Apostles' Creed, by Joan Chittister, a Benedictine nun and theologian. One morning, I came to this arresting paragraph, where Chittister writes:

> ...I found myself doing graduate work in Communication Theory at the very moment in academic history when philosophers, semanticists, and psychologists began to agree that thought does not shape language, *language shapes thought*. The words I use, in other words, determine the thoughts I think—about myself, about the world, *about life and all its relationships*, including my relationship with God and God's relationship to us. The thought began to burrow into my soul like grass cracking cement. [*Emphasis mine*]

That thought burrowed its way into my own soul in the same way as it had Chittister's. But for me that morning, the focus of the thought was the phrase "domestic partnership." When I said those words, I thought of a legal contract between two persons whose connection is (simply?) that they share the same domicile. Or my God, I thought, Mary and I could be the Molly Maids, a couple of domestics who just happen to be in business together! When I said the word "marriage," my reaction, instantly, was different. Tears came to my eyes. I thought of the depth, the body, soul, and heart connection we share, a covenant to be here for and with each other and our families for the rest of our lives. I began to understand the significance of standing up in front of our community and claiming our love as married. I thought how special it would be to call Mary my spouse.

Back in the State Senate chamber gallery, we don the Washington United for Marriage T-shirts that are handed out as people arrive. We read, look around, chat with other early birds. We are joined at 4:30 by a couple of friends. We take turns going out to the hall for snacks, down the hall to the bathroom. I am jumpy.

Below us, senators begin strolling calmly to their desks. The galleries are packed by now; the halls outside, too, are crowded with witnesses and no longer quiet. At 6:00 the Senate is called to order and receives a motion to be at ease while the parties meet in caucus. When they return, several amendments to SB 6239 are introduced and voted on. And then comes the debate on the bill itself. It is respectful, thoughtful, heartfelt. Everyone knows the bill will pass—earlier this week a holdout senator had announced she would cast the deciding twenty-fifth yes vote—so this is an opportunity for different voices to be heard, both in favor of and opposed to marriage equality. The gallery has been warned not to make any audible responses to the debate. The air has that suck-air silence, loaded with emotion. Mary and I alternately hold our breath, nudge each other, reach for the other's hand—or for our Kleenex—as we listen.

> *We ask you for your support tonight because marriage is how society says you are a family. We, like you, seek the chance to live our lives, to experience joy, to care for our families....*
>
> *Passage of this bill will create a hostile environment in the state. It will lead to the silencing of those who believe in traditional marriage....*
>
> *This issue is personal for me. I am the son of a gay father....*
>
> *I'm a Christian. I love all people. I do not judge anyone. And I need to ask your forgiveness as I oppose this bill....*
>
> *I can't deny others the right to have the same richness that I have with my wife....*
>
> *There was a time when men saw women as chattel, a time when white persons saw black persons as slaves. Traditions change....*
>
> *I was in the army for twenty years, and am now in the national guard. There are 66,000 gays in the armed forces today. How can I look at my gay comrades if I vote no on this bill?...*
>
> *The Bill of Rights includes the right to the pursuit of happiness, and happiness includes marriage....*

Finally, it is time for the vote. The tally is twenty-eight in favor, twenty-one opposed. The ayes have it! The chamber galleries erupt in cheers. Everyone is hugging—staff people, visitors, all of us for whom this matters so much. Most have tears in their eyes, as do we.

Mary and I turn to each other. Embracing her, I murmur into her hair, "Will you marry me?"

"Yes," she answers, and I hear the laugh in her voice. "Will *you* marry *me*?"

Acknowledgments

MAMACITA, (read the note on top of a glass preserves jar my daughter gave me for my 70th birthday)
THIS IS YOUR LIFE! ... if you care to tell it ...
Inside this jar are 101 questions about your life, from childhood through today. Dip in to answer one any time you feel like writing up a story from your life. Some are quite personal, so if you want to keep your writing private, that's fine. But I am interested in whatever you want to share. I love you, and I want to hear your stories. Love, Katie

That gift reconnected me with my love of writing, was the impetus for two years of joyful remembrance, and catapulted me onto the path that led to *The Last of the Good Girls*. For that, from the bottom of my heart: thank you, Katie.

Judith Barrington, poet and memoirist, was one of the first and most impactful of many poetry teachers with whom I've studied. Her admonition to "write the truth. . . . [a]nd then write the truth beneath the truth" is a call to integrity that still challenges me, and I owe her credit for whatever rings true in my words.

To Christina Baldwin's workshop, *The Self as the Source of the Story*, in June, 2010; and the 2011 winter writing circle comprised of

Christina, the late Diane Bonne, Anna Singh Deo, Mary Kay (M.K.) Sandford, Kate Stivers, the late Davison Stivers, and Mary Sullivan; I credit both the inspiration and also the push to turn my "glass preserves jar" writing and some of my lifelong output of poetry into a book. Christina took me and my story under her wing, gifted me with the book's title, and has been an invaluable companion and coach every step of the way.

My very earliest, and most thorough, reader was the late Beverly Anderson Forbes—and all of her friends will understand how hard it is to put "the late" by her name. Bev went through my first and several subsequent drafts with a fine-tooth comb. She entered into an enthusiastic dialogue with my manuscript, raised thoughtful questions, offered editorial comments, and pointed out flaws with extraordinary tact and curiosity, always with an eye to helping me hone my message, always in a spirit of support for my writing journey. I wish she could see the product of our work.

A large group of readers gifted me by spending time with my manuscript/s as *The Last of the Good Girls* evolved. They told me what worked for them and what didn't and offered suggestions when more clarity or expansion would benefit the telling of my story. Each of these persons was instrumental in enhancing the quality of the writing, and I'm grateful to them: Christina Baldwin, Barbara Barbee-Pelzel, Rita Bresnahan, Barbara Hager, Jean Hager, Carol Kelly, Mary Anne Knoll, Kristie Langlow, Deborah Nedelman, Burry Pelzel, M. K. Sandford, Mary Sullivan, Marian Svinth, Vivian Unterweger, Kate Wehr, Jim Woodruff, Katie Woodruff, and Dori Jones Yang.

Many others have read and commented on my manuscript in its later stages, warming my heart with their generous responses. Thanks to: Gary Bocz, Sally and Wally Campbell, Sally Cary, Tony Copes, Janet DeWater, Ginny Hager, Mary Hickey, Judith Lonnquist, Betsy Lord, David Maxwell, Jinny McCarty, Jim Patten, Trish Rogers, Ilene Schwartz, Susan Scott, Susan Sever, Jackie Tanner, Bob Woodruff, and Sue Yates.

I'm indebted to Dori Jones Yang, whose open-hearted sharing of her own experience turned her into my publishing coach and made me the beneficiary of her wisdom. Dory connected me to Kathy Campbell, cover, logo and book designer extraordinaire, whose skill and commitment made my book the beauty it is.

No book gets far without endorsements. I am so, so appreciative of Christina Baldwin, Chris Glaser, Tricia Dykers Koenig, Alene Moris, and Janie Spahr for their tangible support of my storytelling.

I've already acknowledged my family in the dedication. The place each of them has in my heart is a treasure beyond words. I want, however, to extend a special, tender word to Mary, my partner for the last fifteen years, who has been my constant companion during the entire process of creating this book. Lovingly, she stayed away when I needed space, gave comfort when I needed it, and cheered me all the way. In addition, she did me the great honor of marrying me on February 10th of this year. *Te amo, mi esposa.*

Mary Ann Woodruff

June 20, 2013

Made in the USA
Charleston, SC
11 September 2013